Mobilizing Communities

Mobilizing Communities

Asset Building as a Community Development Strategy

Edited by
Gary Paul Green and
Ann Goetting

TEMPLE UNIVERSITY PRESS
Philadelphia

TEMPLE UNIVERSITY PRESS
Philadelphia, Pennsylvania 19122
www.temple.edu/tempress

Copyright © 2010 by Temple University
All rights reserved
Published 2010
Paperback edition published 2013

Library of Congress Cataloging-in-Publication Data

Mobilizing communities : asset building as a community development
strategy / edited by Gary Paul Green and Ann Goetting.
    p. cm.
    Includes bibliographical references and index.
    ISBN 978-1-4399-0086-4 (cloth : alk. paper)   1. Community
development—Case studies.   2. Economic development—Case studies.
3. Rural development—Case studies.   4. Community organizations—
Case studies.   I. Green, Gary P.   II. Goetting, Ann.
    HN49.C6M63 2010
    307.1'4120973—dc22

                                                        2009026111

ISBN 978-1-4399-0087-1 (paperback : alk. paper)
ISBN 978-1-4399-0088-8 (e-book)

Printed in the United States of America

091013-P

■■ Contents
■■

Mobilizing Communities

Community Assets

Building the Capacity for Development

GARY PAUL GREEN

Communities are facing new and more powerful challenges to their survival. Globalization threatens the economic base of many of them. International markets create new competition among localities for capital investments and generate pressures to lower labor costs. Globalization also makes it more difficult for communities to plan for the future because of the mobility of capital and labor. In many respects, globalization reflects a new stage in the process by which communities have become integrated into the larger society and economy over the past century (Warren 1978).

Other social and economic changes also make it more challenging for communities to tackle their problems. Urban sprawl undermines the uniqueness of place and promotes class and racial segregation. Sprawl and segregation combine to weaken democracy and civic participation (Oliver 2001). Gentrification makes it more difficult for the poor to obtain affordable housing. Low-income residents are driven out of their neighborhoods because they cannot afford to pay the higher tax assessments. The high rate of immigration during the past two decades has expanded the demand for social services and generates challenges to civic participation (Putnam 2007).

Many communities continue to be burdened by concentrated poverty (Wilson 1996). High rates of poverty create numerous obstacles for residents in these neighborhoods. Inhabitants of poor communities have limited access to basic services such as banking and shopping. Poor communities tend to have a disproportionate number of environmental problems. Youth often lack good role models in poor neighborhoods because the middle class has moved to areas that are safer and that provide better education and housing. Without these role models, they often lack the aspirations for and understanding of a wider range of opportunities. Limited social networks in poor neighborhoods tend to restrict the available job information and contacts that provide employment opportunities for the poor (Tigges, Browne, and Green 1998).

As these forces present new challenges to communities, political changes place more responsibilities for social and economic welfare at the local level. Federal and state governments are devolving many of their responsibilities onto local governments and community-based organizations, which are increasingly becoming responsible for providing social services, addressing housing needs, and implementing welfare programs. In addition, because of the fiscal pressures on local governments, localities are now making a more intensive effort to promote economic growth (Fleischmann, Green, and Kwong 1992). Do community-based organizations have sufficient resources to address these issues? Can they overcome the powerful influence of the local elites? How can organizations effectively build public participation in their programs? Is it possible for communities to effectively overcome the broader social and economic forces affecting them? In this book, we explore how effectively community-based organizations are responding to these challenges.

Interest in community-based development has grown over the past two decades, primarily because of interest in devolving government authority. Devolution requires that residents design and implement programs on a wide variety of issues, such as welfare reform, housing, health care, and environmental protection. Cuts in the federal budget have shifted the responsibilities for funding and implementing many programs to the states and localities. Yet concerns remain that most communities do not have the capacity to take on these responsibilities. Some critics charge that community-based development is often co-opted by local elites (Logan and Molotch 1987). Others contend that it is difficult for community-based development efforts to maintain control because they must rely on outside resources, especially for financial and technical assistance (Stone 1982).

Many communities look to external resources to address these challenges. These resources might include financial assistance, investments by businesses, or technical expertise. Outside resources are attractive because they offer the potential of a "quick fix" or address a perceived local deficiency. Dependence on external resources, however, raises numerous problems for community development. One such problem is that it may inhibit communities from cultivating the capacity to address their own needs. In his book *The Careless Society*, John McKnight (1995) argues that technical assistance from professionals creates dependency. Technical assistance is premised on the assumption that the community has a problem and the professional has the answer. Professionalized service creates clients who are in need of continued care. This relationship, McKnight argues, works against community capacity building.

Looking outside for resources and assistance can create additional problems. Technical assistance may not match the need in the local setting. Providers of technical assistance frequently have a generic response to community issues. They have little, if any, knowledge or understanding of the local context. Professional training and experience is based on general processes and issues that need to be interpreted and translated at the local level. It takes time to understand the community context and the social dynamics that might influence the success of community interventions.

And just as important, technical-assistance providers seldom are able to offer follow-up support. Continued support is critical to the success of community development (Pulver and Dodson 1992). The professional model of technical assistance typically lacks this element. Technical assistance is usually characterized by delivery of a product or service that is limited in time. Most community projects take much more time and commitment than outside experts are able to provide. Typically, experts do not live in the community and spend little time on implementing and monitoring interventions.

During the 1990s, an alternative model of community development emerged that emphasized the importance of building on community assets rather than focusing on needs and problems. John Kretzmann and John McKnight (1993) are credited with being the architects of this new approach. Their work in the inner city of Chicago as well as in numerous other communities suggested that most neighborhoods, even the poorest ones, have important resources that can serve as the springboard for community action. Many other foundations, organizations, and institutions have adopted the asset-based development approach. For example, the Ford Foundation established "Asset Building and Community Development" as one of three core programs. The Search Institute and others have identified asset-based development as the key foundation of their work. Numerous books and workbooks have been written on asset-based development (Fisher 2003; Green and Haines 2007).

Jody Kretzmann and John McKnight (1993) define assets as the gifts, skills, and capacities of individuals, associations, and institutions within a community. Many times these resources are overlooked and ignored by residents as they attempt to improve the quality of life. Asset-based development involves a process of identifying and mobilizing these resources to achieve collective goals.

This book provides several case studies of community-based asset development in several different contexts. Although the asset model has been widely adopted, there is very little research evaluating its effectiveness. The goal of this book is to provide insights into how these asset-based development efforts can work more effectively. We review these asset-based development approaches and summarize some of the lessons learned from these experiences in different contexts and with different foci.

Community Assets

Emphasizing assets—rather than needs—represents a transformation in how community development practitioners have approached their work over the past two decades. Community needs usually include issues such as unemployment, poverty, crime, and lack of affordable housing. Organizing residents around these needs can be a powerful way to address inequities and powerlessness. In many respects, the history of community development is premised on the idea that it is possible to build communities by acting collectively to address local needs. Identifying needs can provide a strong motivation for residents to gain a more powerful voice through collective action. Saul Alinsky's (1969) approach to community development was to begin with small problems and organize residents around the issues in order to demonstrate the power in community mobilization. Needs assessment, then, has been a valued element of the community development toolbox among practitioners (Johnson et al. 1987).

Needs assessment as a model for community development, however, has several drawbacks. Focusing on problems may make it difficult to establish long-term partnerships and coalitions to improve the quality of life in the community. Collective action focusing on problems is usually not based on a clear vision of the goals of community residents. This disconnect can lead to episodic efforts rather than sustained collective action. Once the issue is addressed, it is difficult to continue to energize residents and focus on new projects and issues. Partnerships and coalitions established for a specific issue may erode if organizers shift to new needs. Establishing a formal community organization can be difficult to do on a needs basis as well.

Needs assessment can often lead to a sense of powerlessness or alienation, or both, as residents become overwhelmed by the complexity and difficulty of community problems. This is especially the case when residents diagnose the causes of their problems as structural forces that operate outside their community. If unemployment is defined as a result of corporate decision making in response to global market opportunities, it is easy for residents to become alienated and focus on individual responses. Even when the local power structure and public officials are considered the source of the community problems, it may be overwhelming for residents to see how they can bring about the necessary political change.

Finally, needs assessment often lends itself to relying on outsiders to help solve community problems. In many cases, communities even turn to outsiders to conduct the needs assessment to tell them what their most serious concerns and problems are. As McKnight (1995) suggests, it is in the interests of professionals and technical-assistance providers to promote this dependency. Communities frequently turn to outside assistance because they believe the issues or problems are too complex for local residents. This type of assistance does very little to help build community capacity (Chaskin et al. 2001). It is possible, however, for professionals and technical-assistance providers to empower local residents. This might mean helping residents develop the research skills, substantive knowledge, or both, to address community issues.

Asset-based development begins with a much different premise. It is initiated by mapping the key strengths or available resources in the community. Individuals, organizations, and institutions have resources that can be used to enhance the quality of life for residents. Another way of thinking about assets is to consider them as different forms of community capital, including financial, social, physical, environmental, human, political, and cultural capital (Green and Haines 2007). These assets are considered capital because investments in them generate additional resources or benefits for the community. This is most clearly the case with financial capital. Wealth in the community can be used to create additional wealth for residents. Investments in other forms of community capital also generate benefits for residents. The key, however, is that these investment are made locally. This does not mean that the profit motive is removed from the process. Instead, social objectives are added to the profit motive.

This concept of community capital is not limited to finance. Investments in other forms of community capital can also yield collective benefits. Efforts to protect and manage natural resources can produce important community benefits. Similarly, public investments in housing, cultural amenities, and education generate important community-wide benefits.

In many cases, the focus of asset building is on how organizations and institutions can better serve residents. Rather than providing training for jobs that workers must take elsewhere, training is matched to jobs that can be created locally. Similarly, if an absentee-owned firm processes natural resources, many of the benefits often flow outside the community. The same thing may occur if families place their savings in banks and other financial institutions that invest these resources in other localities. When assets are owned and controlled by residents and invested in local projects, they are more likely to generate benefits for the community.

Asset building addresses many institutional obstacles to the development of places that cannot be adequately addressed through individual action. Community-based organizations can overcome many of the collective-action problems associated with community development. For example, while individual employers in a community may lack skilled workers, they may be reluctant to invest in training because they fear they may lose these workers after they receive the training. Similarly, individual employers may not have the resources to provide the necessary training programs. Groups of employers who have common needs, however, may build collective programs that address these issues. Community development offers collective solutions to these problems by building on the existing resources within the community.

Mobilizing Assets

Kretzmann and McKnight (1993) identify several steps in mobilizing community assets. The first stage is identifying the capacities of residents, organizations, and institutions. The idea that all individuals have the capacity to contribute to their community is fundamental to this approach. We often overlook the potential contributions of youth, senior citizens, and people with disabilities. In addition to standard labor-market skills and experiences, we need to know about volunteer activities, hobbies, and care-giving experiences. One of the obstacles is that residents often do not think of many of their interests and experiences as an asset that can contribute to their community's well-being.

Community development practitioners obtain much of this information on individuals through a variety of methods, including one-on-one and peer-to-peer interviews, group interviews, self-administered inventories, and community events (Kretzmann, McKnight, and Sheehan 1997). This capacity inventory needs to identify the gifts and potential contributions of all residents and to focus on solutions, not problems.

Associations and organizations are composed of important social relationships or social capital that can be valuable to community development. Asset-based development usually involves mapping both formal and informal organizations in the community. Formal organizations are usually visible, and there are directories that help identify them. Informal organizations—such as block clubs, neighborhood watches, or garden clubs—however, usually do not show up on any formal lists because they are not incorporated or they do not have any paid staff. Identifying these networks and social relationships can help organize residents to build coalitions and power in the community.

Information on informal networks and organizations is typically collected through the same methods used to identify individual assets.

Community institutions—such as schools, hospitals, and libraries—are potentially important resources for community development. These institutions purchase goods and services that could contribute to the local economy. They have facilities that can be used for community events. Many local institutions could potentially hire workers in the area. Mapping these institutions involves assessing the institutional assets with the goal of identifying resources that could contribute to community building.

After mapping the assets, community organizers build relationships across the community that will help implement the goals and vision of the project. Mobilizing assets requires broad support. The asset-based development approach relies on leveraging local resources to gain outside support as well. Although it is important to build from local resources, it is also important to tap into existing outside resources that will enhance those assets.

Asset-based development is not without its critics. It has been accused of ignoring power relations within communities. It may be the case that asset-building approaches tend to be less conflict oriented than many other community-organizing approaches. Asset-based development emphasizes common interests and values that can serve as a basis for mobilizing residents to address the critical issues facing their communities. This often means that organizers are setting aside some of the issues that may divide the community. There is nothing inherent in the approach, however, that averts conflict with the power elite. Nor does the emphasis on common interests ignore conflict. But asset-based development does seek to overcome racial, gender, and class differences that frequently constrain community development projects.

Another possible criticism is that it is more difficult to mobilize communities around assets than it might be around needs and problems. It probably is easier to bring residents together around a problem or need, but it may be more difficult to sustain that effort. Also, residents typically want to jump to solutions before adequately understanding the nature of the problem or issue. In the long run, mobilizing communities to understand their local resources can be a more effective strategy for improving their quality of life.

The Case Studies

The chapters solicited for this volume identify factors influencing the success of community-based asset development. Literally hundreds of community-based organizations are using the asset-based development approach, and this book provides both a conceptual framework and practical guidance to community development practitioners. We brought together a unique set of practitioners and academics in the community development field. We have solicited case studies from a wide variety of geographical settings. In addition, we have included case studies of asset-based development among different racial and ethnic groups. Each author was asked to address some common issues and questions:

1. What is the context or setting for the case study?
2. What factors contributed to the initiation of the project?
3. How successful was the asset-based approach in promoting public participation in the project?
4. How were the key assets identified?
5. Were local assets leveraged for outside resources? If so, how?
6. What role did the local government and other public institutions play in the project?
7. What were the outcomes and impacts of the projects?
8. What are the chief lessons to be learned from this experience?

Not all the case studies included in this volume involved a formal asset-mapping process. A formal process might entail a community-wide effort to map assets, develop a set of goals, and mobilize residents to implement programs. All the cases, however, do include communities that recognize the importance of local assets and develop strategies to enhance the quality of life by using these resources.

Sarah Dewees and Stewart Sarkozy-Banoczy (Chapter 2) provide a look at community development financial institutions (CDFIs) on three Indian reservations: the Citizen Potawatomi Nation in Shawnee, Oklahoma; the Lac Courte Oreilles Ojibwe Band on the Lac Courte Oreilles Reservation in Hayward, Wisconsin; and the Cheyenne River Sioux Tribe on the Cheyenne River Reservation in Eagle Butte, South

Dakota. There has been a rapid expansion of CDFIs; currently there are forty-four Native CDFIs and another sixty-six emerging ones. These institutions not only focus on access to credit, but they play a critical role in building the financial skills required to manage small businesses and to expand existing businesses. Their analysis of three different CDFIs suggests that "right" sized credit needs to be supplemented with training, technical assistance, and financial education.

Emily Blejwas (Chapter 3) examines the role of the arts in asset-based development in the rural South. There is a growing recognition that the arts can play an important role in community and economic development. In her case study of a Black Belt community, Blejwas points to some obstacles, especially race, involved in mobilizing assets in this region. Segregation prompts a lack of trust and communication in implementing asset-based development. By consciously promoting inclusive participation in the community, this arts-based project attempted to overcome some of the racial barriers that have existed for decades in the community. Blejwas provides a specific set of recommendations for mobilizing assets in a racially segregated community.

Michael Dougherty and Rocio Peralta (Chapter 4) analyze a community-based effort in Guatemala that focused on the community's environmental capital. Their case study of the failed attempt to designate the Laguna Chichoj region as a protected area demonstrates some of the obstacles unique to mobilizing assets in developing countries. In particular, the weakness of civil society in these contexts makes it extremely difficult for communities to benefit from amenity-based development. They conclude that the multifunctionality of environmental capital in rural communities undermines genuine community initiatives in a developing economy. A strong institutional context is required to benefit local residents effectively. Without this strong institutional context, it is difficult for community initiatives to manage and control these development projects. The case study also involves indigenous groups that lacked sufficient political power in this context.

Rhonda Phillips and Gordon Shockley (Chapter 5) explore cultural capital as a community asset. Building on David Throsby's work, they define cultural capital as comprising both tangible and intangible manifestations of culture. Tangible goods might include buildings, paintings, sculptures, or other products that have cultural significance.

Intangible cultural capital typically includes cultural practices and traditions that help bind individuals to a group. Phillips and Shockley discuss an arts-based economic-development project in Bellows Falls, Vermont that adopted various strategies for promoting the arts in the region. They argue that arts-based development projects are most successful when they are combined with efforts to build other assets in the community.

John Kretzmann and Deborah Puntenney (Chapter 6) review two successful asset-building cases in the City of Chicago. The Westside Health Authority (WHA) and Bethel New Life (BNL) are two of the more effective groups working in the city. BNL began in a small Lutheran church in West Garfield Park in the early 1980s and has evolved into a comprehensive community development corporation. WHA also was created in the 1980s and has evolved into a community organization with a budget of more than $3 million. Both of these organizations operate in communities that have experienced significant losses in population and businesses and have seen growth in unemployment and crime rates. Part of the success of these organizations has been their ability to identify and train local leaders, who have been effective at engaging marginalized residents in neighborhood-revitalization efforts.

In a case of amenity-based development, Gary Paul Green (Chapter 7) focuses on some of the tensions between growth and development in a rural context. Petoskey, Michigan is a community that historically has had an economy based on extracting natural resources. As its economy becomes based more on tourism and recreation, it experiences the types of pressures that threaten the small-town atmosphere and the natural amenities that make it an attractive place to live and work. Managing growth can be challenging because of the conflicting interests between full-time and seasonal residents in the community. The community has successfully avoided some of the traps associated with a tourism economy by promoting year-round employment and diversifying its economic base.

Mark Harvey and Lionel Beaulieu (Chapter 8) discuss the role of resident participation in two community development initiatives in the Mississippi Delta. Their comparative analysis demonstrates how community participation can be enhanced through strong leadership and organizational support. This study challenges some of the previous work on asset-based development that downplays the importance of professionalization and leadership in grassroots efforts. Their analysis does suggest, however, that it is possible to meld strong organizational development and participatory development.

In the last chapter (Chapter 9), Gary Paul Green identifies some of the conceptual themes in the case studies and examines some of the implications for the practice of community development. Key themes include the difficulty of mobilizing across racial and ethnic lines, the multifunctionality of and interrelationships among community assets, and the significance of professionalization and organizational capacity. He also discusses the implications of these case studies for practitioners and the need for future research on this topic.

References

Alinsky, Saul D. 1969. *Reveille for Radicals*. New York: Random House.

Chaskin, Robert J., Prudence Brown, Sudhir Venkatesh, and Avis Vidal. 2001. *Building Community Capacity*. New York: Aldine de Gruyter.

Fisher, Deborah. 2003. *Assets in Action: A Handbook for Making Communities Better Places to Grow Up*. Minneapolis, MN: Search Institute.

Fleischmann, Arnold, Gary P. Green, and Tsz Man Kwong. 1992. "What's a city to do? Explaining differences in local economic development policies." *Western Political Quarterly* 45:677–699.

Green, Gary Paul, and Anna Haines. 2007. *Asset Building and Community Development,* 2nd Edition. Thousand Oaks, CA: Sage Publications.

Johnson, Donald E., Larry R. Meiller, Lorna Clancy Miller, and Gene F. Summers. 1987. *Needs Assessment: Theory and Methods*. Ames: Iowa State University Press.

Kretzmann, John, and John McKnight. 1993. *Building Communities from the Inside Out: A Path Toward Finding and Mobilizing a Community's Assets*. Evanston, IL: Center for Urban Affairs and Policy Research, Northwestern University.

Kretzmann, John P., John L. McKnight, and Geralyn Sheehan. 1997. *A Guide to Capacity Inventories: Mobilizing the Community Skills of Local Residents*. Evanston, IL: Center for Urban Affairs and Policy Research, Northwestern University.

Logan, John R., and Harvey L. Molotch. 1987. *Urban Fortunes: The Political Economy of Place*. Berkeley: University of California Press.

McKnight, John. 1995. *The Careless Society: Community and Its Counterfeits*. New York: Basic Books.

Oliver, J. Eric. 2001. *Democracy in Suburbia*. Princeton, NJ: Princeton University Press.

Pulver, Glen, and David Dodson. 1992. *Designing Development Strategies in Small Towns.* Washington, DC: The Aspen Institute.

Putnam, Robert. 2007. "E Pluribus Unum." *Scandinavia Political Studies* 30:137–174.

Stone, Clarence N. 1982. "Social stratification, non-decision-making and the study of community power." *American Politics Quarterly* 10:275–302.

Tigges, Leann M., Irene Browne, and Gary P. Green. 1998. "Social isolation of the urban poor: Race, class, and neighborhood effects on social resources." *The Sociological Quarterly* 39:53–77.

Warren, Roland L. 1978. *The Community in America,* 3rd Edition. Chicago, IL: Rand McNally College Publishing Company.

Wilson, William Julius. 1996. *When Work Disappears: The World of the New Urban Poor.* New York: Alfred A. Knopf.

2 Investing in the Double Bottom Line

Growing Financial Institutions in Native Communities

SARAH DEWEES AND
STEWART SARKOZY-BANOCZY

Introduction

In the past twenty years, more and more tribal governments and Native-led nonprofit organizations have mobilized to address the multifaceted economic challenges facing their communities. These efforts represent an innovative way to begin to repair the damage wrought by years of colonial and postcolonial control of Indian communities in North America. Yet they also represent an important model of economic development— one that mobilizes local institutions to create local solutions to respond to the changes in global capital markets and the increasing flow of capital and other resources away from rural areas. This chapter focuses on one type of institution that is facing the challenge of financial markets head-on: local community development financial institutions (CDFIs). Increasingly, CDFIs are locating on reservations and in Native communities to inject capital into the local economy, provide culturally appropriate financial education and other technical assistance, and stimulate economic development.

Economic Development in Native Communities

Approaches to economic development in Native communities are as diverse as the communities themselves. There are over 560 federally recognized tribes in the United States, with populations ranging from a few hundred to nearly two hundred thousand. Some tribes own a large land base, the most notable being the seventeen-million-acre Navajo Nation, and others own only a few acres of ancestral homeland. The geography of federally recognized Indian tribes also differs. Some tribes, including the Salt River Pima Maricopa Indian Community, have a reservation very near a large metropolitan area, and other tribes, including the Turtle Mountain Band of Chippewa Indians, are located in remote rural areas, isolated from markets and services. There is also great diversity in the indigenous people of Alaska and Hawaii, as well as the non-federally-recognized tribal communities—all of whom bring their own unique cultural, geographic, economic, and social variables into the mix.

Despite the tremendous diversity of Native nations and their environments for economic development, some themes emerge when analyzing the key opportunities and challenges (Cornell and Kalt 1997; Dewees and Sarkozy-Banoczy 2007; Dewees and Sarkozy-Banoczy 2009; Hillabrant et al. 2004). It has been documented that Native communities face many barriers related to access to credit and financial services (Hillabrant et al. 2004; Malkin 2003; Malkin 2004). The reasons for this are numerous and include the fact that there are few financial institutions physically located on reservations, lender perceptions that Indian communities are not good markets for credit, and an inability to use trust land for collateral.[1]

In 2001 the CDFI Fund of the U.S. Treasury published the *Native American Lending Study* and documented what many working in Indian Country already knew—that a lack of private-sector financial institutions within Native communities has significantly hindered access to credit and capital for business development and other economic activity (Community Development Financial Institutions Fund 2001). That study found that the majority of respondents identified one significant factor as the source of economic and social challenges being faced by Native communities: a lack of access to capital and financial services. According to the report, nearly two-thirds of Native American and Native Hawaiian respondents reported that business loans, private-equity investments, and conventional mortgages for Native business owners are "difficult" to "impossible" to achieve. Home equity loans, construction loans, and property rehabilitation loans are also in short supply on Indian lands and Hawaiian homelands. Only recently have some banks begun lending to tribal members on some reservations, and problems persist related to an inability to foreclose on some loans because of legal issues related to sovereignty and lack of Uniform Commercial Codes on reservations.[2]

Many Native communities are not seen as good markets for financial services because of high poverty levels and perceived low levels of financial literacy (Malkin 2003, 2004; Meeks 2006). Many structural factors have contributed to low financial literacy in Native communities. These factors include a lack of access to banking services, fewer role models in families, a history of poverty, cultural beliefs that value generosity over savings, a history of low levels of financial education, and geographic isolation (Dewees 2004a, 2004b, 2004c; Edwards and Schultz 2007; Malkin 2003; Malkin 2004; Meeks 2006). The National Credit Union Foundation (NCUF) recently held a summit to identify best practices to serve Native Americans. In a report from that summit, authored by the Native American Credit Union Initiative, the NCUF stated that the majority of the credit unions they surveyed identified low financial literacy as a challenge for the Native American population with whom they work (Jaure 2006). A 2004 study of financial education among Native American youth conducted by the Jump$tart Coalition found that Native youth consistently rank near the bottom of the four major test areas: income, money management, savings, and spending (Jorgenson and Mandell 2007).

Asset Building in Native Communities

The concept of asset-based development, particularly focused on financial assets, has received increased recognition in policy and program development circles over the past fifteen years. In 1991, Michael Sherraden published his book *Assets and the Poor* (Sherraden 1991), marking the beginning of heightened public debate on the topic of asset-based social-welfare policy. Social-welfare policy in the United

States, Sherraden argued, has focused on income maintenance without providing the poor with real economic ladders out of poverty. At the same time, asset limitations and disincentives for asset ownership effectively block the poor from working toward owning a home, starting a small business, or finding other asset-based paths out of poverty. While our tax system provides asset-ownership incentives to middle- and higher-income people through tax breaks for home owners and small-business owners, the poor receive no such support. Only when we provide opportunities for asset ownership to the poor, Sherraden has argued, will our social-welfare system in the United States begin to be truly equitable (see also Boshara 2001).

Sherraden (1991:155) defines asset building as "accumulated resources that are invested for social and economic development." These investments can be in human, social, or tangible assets, most often in small-business development, education, and home ownership. According to leading scholars on asset development, increasing people's assets, as opposed to just their incomes, has significant economic, psychological, and social benefits (Ford Foundation N.d.; Sherraden 1991; Sherraden 2003). Not only does small-business ownership increase incomes, but it increases hope for the future, pride, and economic self-determination (Sherraden, Sanders, and Sherraden 2003). Sherraden (1991:155–156) argues,

> People think and behave differently when they are accumulating assets, and the world responds to them differently as well. More specifically, assets improve economic stability; connect people with a viable, hopeful future; stimulate development of human and other capital; enable people to focus and specialize; provide a foundation for risk taking; yield personal, social, and political dividends; and enhance the welfare of offspring.

Citing the impact of asset ownership for the poor, Sherraden (1991) has advocated new policy models specific to building the financial assets of the poor, including small-business development, Individual Development Accounts (IDAs), increased home ownership, children's savings accounts, and other plans to lift people out of poverty, move them from a state of dependence to independence, and provide them with choices and a vision for the future.

The field of asset-building policy has only recently addressed the economic challenges present in Native communities in the United States. Native people and their communities and economies possess a unique history of colonial and postcolonial asset stripping, a history faced by few other communities in the United States (Adamson, Black, and Dewees 2003; Hicks et al. 2005; Lui et al. 2006). In addition, some argue that Native communities ascribe value to assets and wealth in ways that are different from mainstream western economic models (Hertel et al. 2008; Hicks et al. 2005). In some Native communities, asset accumulation is appropriate only if it supports traditional notions of sharing resources with the collective group and providing for others (Adamson, Black, and Dewees 2003; Hicks et al. 2005). Others have observed that asset building in some Native communities may focus on short-term needs, including repairing credit or purchasing a vehicle to get to work, rather than long-term goals such as starting a small business or purchasing a home (Hicks et al. 2005).

Another challenge is the fact that many Native communities lack the financial, legal, physical, and even social infrastructure that is needed to support private-sector economic development (Dewees and Sarkozy-Banoczy 2009). Largely because of the history of underdevelopment and federal control of Indian affairs, many tribal governments are still working to establish the legal systems that promote private-enterprise development and support the effective functioning of economic markets. In addition, because of the unique legal challenges associated with the federal control of trust land, many of the basic components of the economic and legal systems needed to support small-business ownership, home ownership, and other asset-building strategies are not present in many Native communities (Dewees and Sarkozy-Banoczy 2009; Hicks et al. 2005).

Despite these differences, many argue that asset-building policies and programs have a place in economic-development plans for Native communities if they are presented in a culturally appropriate manner (Adamson, Black, and Dewees 2003; Carr 2006; Dewees and Florio 2003; Dewees and Sarkozy-Banoczy 2007; Hicks et al. 2005; King et al. 2003; Miller 2001). Over the past ten years, an increasing number of Native communities have been using IDA programs, small-business development centers, and community loan funds to stimulate economic development in reservation-based communities (Adamson, Black, and Dewees 2003; Dewees and Florio 2003; Dewees and Sarkozy-Banoczy 2007).

CDFI Development in Native Communities

CDFIs are specialized financial institutions that work in market niches that have not been adequately served by traditional financial institutions. CDFIs can provide a wide range of financial products and services, including commercial loans to start or expand small businesses, financial services needed by low-income households, and mortgage financing for first-time home buyers. In addition, these institutions provide services that help ensure that credit is used effectively, such as technical assistance to small businesses and financial education and credit counseling to consumers. CDFIs contribute directly to asset building in communities by helping people buy a home or start or expand a small business. CDFIs also contribute indirectly to asset building by helping people gain the financial skills necessary to manage credit, run a small business successfully, and scale up their small business when the time comes.

CDFIs include community development banks, credit unions, loan funds, and microenterprise loan funds. Nationwide, there are over eight hundred CDFIs or CDFI-like organizations, and the U.S. Treasury has certified over 774 of them. A CDFI can become certified by the U.S. Treasury if it meets certain criteria for management of staff, financial systems, and programs. Certification by the U.S. Treasury is an advantage because it allows these CDFIs to receive one-to-one matched financial assistance from the U.S. Department of Treasury CDFI Fund. Certification has also become a stepping stone to maturity that funders, partners, and others in community development now recognize. A CDFI, however, does not have to be certified to provide services in a local community.

As recently as 2000, there were only six Native CDFIs serving reservation-based communities. Over the past decade the field of Native CDFIs has exploded as more and more tribal governments and community leaders have identified CDFIs as a successful model for contributing to asset building and economic development in Native communities. As of May 2008, there were forty-seven Native CDFIs certified by the CDFI Fund and 129 additional emerging Native

CDFIs throughout the country (Carr 2006; Dewees and Sarkoczy 2009; Schneider et al. 2007).

Contributions of CDFIs to Native and Reservation-Based Communities

Native CDFIs contribute to asset building in Native and reservation-based communities in several important ways. They provide access to credit in areas that may have few other financial resources or services available to them. In addition, they provide technical assistance and training to ensure that the credit is used effectively and to increase the financial skills of community members. Through these services, they promote asset building in the form of small-business development. Finally, they contribute to changing the social infrastructure in a community by helping to create a mentor class of small-business owners.

Access to Credit

Native CDFIs address problems related to the lack of financial infrastructure in Native communities and on Indian reservations by providing access to "right-sized" credit that is best suited to the client's needs. CDFIs are unique in that they can offer a broad range of credit products ranging from smaller microloans to larger business loans. Because most CDFIs are nonprofit socially entrepreneurial organizations, they are motivated by community development goals, not just the pursuit of profit. This allows them to offer loans, including starter loans and microloans of $1,000 or less, with smaller profit margins. These loans meet a market need for start-up capital for small businesses while helping individuals get used to handling credit and paying back a loan. They are often credited with providing a "double-bottom-line" payoff—earning a small profit for the CDFI in the collection of interest and also contributing to the "social bottom line" of increasing the financial skills of the borrowers. Many recipients of these loans go on to take out larger loans, sometimes even from mainstream financial institutions. All in all, this results in more money flowing into Native communities for asset building. CDFIs can also provide larger loans if there is demand for them. This tailored approach to lending helps provide each unique Native community with the financial services they need to stimulate asset building and economic development in the form of small-business development and increased home ownership. It also helps develop a class of skilled borrowers who may create a greater demand for credit in Native communities over time.

Technical Assistance and Training

The CDFI model is especially effective because it pairs access to flexible, adaptable credit with ongoing, intensive technical assistance. The services provided by CDFIs in Native communities include basic financial-education classes, IDAs, small-business assistance, and classes on home ownership. Native CDFIs are among the most important institutions for delivering financial education in Native communities, along with tribal colleges and tribal housing authorities. In some cases, clients are required to take a financial-education class before they can access credit from the CDFI. Other CDFIs provide financial education through IDA programs or as part of their business training programs. However financial education is provided, Native CDFIs help create a more financially skilled class of future borrowers on the reservation or in the local community. They also create a "mentor class" that perpetuates the financial and asset-building knowledge curve in the community. Predatory lending on Indian reservations remains a large problem and contributes to asset stripping in many Native communities (Edwards and Schultz 2007; Smith 2003). The financial education offered at Native CDFIs, in addition to providing options for lower-cost credit products, helps combat predatory lending and keep more assets and financial resources in the local community.

Small-Business Development

Development of entrepreneurship is an appropriate strategy for Native communities because it represents a way in which to "plug the leaks" in the local economy, promote economic development through individual empowerment, move away from the dependency model fostered by four hundred years of misguided federal policy, and stimulate private-sector development in what was previously a one-sector economy (Dewees 2004a; Dewees and Sarkozy-Banoczy 2007; Dewees and

Sarkozy-Banoczy 2009; Malkin 2004). Entrepreneurship development is also a key strategy for increasing asset control and asset development in Native communities—whether increasing access to financial assets, developing institutional assets like small businesses in the community, or leveraging existing assets in a way that promotes self-sufficiency (Adamson, Black, and Dewees 2003). A lack of locally owned businesses drains money from the local economy because tribal members are forced to import the vast majority of the goods and services they need from border towns (and even further away), perpetuating cycles of poverty and disenfranchisement (Egan-McKenna and Gabriel 1991). Native CDFIs play a particularly important role in addressing this problem by providing the capital, training, and technical assistance necessary to support the Native-owned businesses that have begun to redirect ownership and control back into the Native and reservation communities. The importance of technical assistance in getting a client ready to access credit and start a business cannot be understated. Ongoing technical assistance is just as critical as the loan is for ensuring that a small-business owner succeeds. Starting a business is not just a data point that measures an outcome—it is actually the beginning of a long process during which a business owner is likely to need continual support and advice (Dewees and Sarkozy-Banoczy 2007; Malkin 2004; Malkin and Aseron 2006a, 2006b).

Contributions to the Social Infrastructure in Native Communities

A fourth impact of Native CDFIs that is often overlooked is their contribution to the social infrastructure of Native communities. The social infrastructure of a community refers to the collection of social norms, networks, and institutions that contribute to the mobilization of community resources for economic development (see, for example, Flora and Flora 1993; Flora et al. 1997). CDFIs have served an important role in changing the social and cultural norms related to small-business development in reservation and other Native communities. The legacy of poverty and colonialism in many Native communities has resulted in low levels of Native business ownership. This is slowly changing, however, as new generations of tribal members starting businesses become comfortable with financial institutions and identify sustainable paths out of poverty. By providing training classes and ongoing technical assistance, CDFIs help produce a business class in the local community, or a group of people who own and manage private businesses and can serve as an example for others (Dewees and Sarkozy-Banoczy 2007; Dewees and Sarkozy-Banoczy 2009). The business owner becomes part of the growing mentor class for his or her family, community, and nation.

Case-Study Analysis

One of the best ways to understand the multifaceted impact of CDFIs working in Native communities is to conduct case studies of several across the nation. Case studies provide a way to use qualitative methodology to test theories and are likely to generate more valid data than quantitative research, although the findings are usually not generalizable to the full population universe (Yin 2002). This chapter will provide case studies of three Native CDFIs: Four Bands Community Fund, serving the Cheyenne River Sioux tribe on the Cheyenne River Reservation in Eagle Butte, South Dakota; Citizen Potawatomi Community Development Corporation (CPCDC), serving the Citizen Potawatomi Nation (CPN) in Shawnee, Oklahoma; and Lac Courte Oreilles Federal Credit Union (LCOFCU), serving the Lac Courte Oreilles Ojibwe Band on the Lac Courte Oreilles Reservation in Hayward, Wisconsin. Case-study data were collected through phone interviews and review of secondary source material. The goal of the case studies is to describe the operations of three CDFIs located in Native communities, identify lessons learned, and explore whether these case-study data support the ideas presented in the literature review herein.

Four Bands Community Fund

Four Bands Community Fund is a 501(c)(3) nonprofit corporation serving the residents of the Cheyenne River Reservation in rural western South Dakota. The Cheyenne River Reservation has a land area approximately the size of Connecticut, with some of the highest poverty figures in the nation. The two counties that make up the Cheyenne

River Reservation, Dewey and Ziebach counties, had poverty rates of 28 percent and 51 percent, respectively, in 2005 (Northwest Area Foundation 2008). Within the tribal reservation boundaries, 42 percent of families with children under the age of eighteen lived below the poverty level in 1999 (U.S. Census 2000). The Cheyenne River Sioux tribe has a population of 8,470 people, according to the 2000 Census, but had a tribal enrollment of 14,666 nationally in 2005 (Tiller 2005). The closest city to the reservation boundary is Pierre, which is ninety-one miles away.

Founded in 2000, Four Bands Community Fund was certified by the CDFI Fund in 2001 and currently offers a variety of loan products and training programs. Four Bands Community Fund's mission is to assist entrepreneurs of the Cheyenne River Indian Reservation with training, business incubation, and access to capital, encouraging economic development and enhancing the quality of life for all communities and residents of the reservation. According to its Web site, Four Bands Community Fund "uses an asset-based approach and provides training and loan funds to enable people to create their own futures" (Four Bands Community Fund 2005).

History

The plan for Four Bands Community Fund was developed late in 1999. The Cheyenne River Sioux tribe first passed a resolution incorporating the organization (there are no tribal corporation codes, so incorporation by resolution was the only option). The passage of the resolution by the tribal council was an important act of support and reflected a long planning and consensus-building process. The development of Four Bands Community Fund was part of an original five-pronged effort of the tribe's economic-development committee and planning department (as of this date, the loan fund is the only one of the five to move forward). A community task force was created in 1999 that included members from the tribe's economic-development committee and planning departments, as well as representatives from the Federal Deposit Insurance Corporation, U.S. Department of Agriculture Rural Development, and the Federal Reserve. This joint development effort provided the support of the tribal government and involvement of community members, but eventually allowed the group to spin off and start its own nonprofit 501(c)(3) corporation, ensuring separation from tribal government politics. Four Bands Community Fund incorporated under state law in 2000 with a mission of providing lending, training, and technical assistance to a community in great need of economic development. The leader of the task force (who eventually became the first executive director) took time to research and develop the market, create the organizational documents, and do the initial fundraising, all with the blessing and support of the tribal council and task force members.

Financial Products

Four Band's programs and services focus on developing private businesses for the reservation, with loan products linked to business training and consulting. Four Bands Community Fund offers loan programs for people who live on the Cheyenne River Reservation and operate the business they are requesting loan funds for within the reservation boundaries. Loan recipients must be either members of the Cheyenne River Sioux tribe or permanent residents on the reservation. Four Bands offers microloans and small-business loans, and in addition has recently started a "credit-builder" loan of up to $2,500 to help a person repair his or her credit history. Before being allowed to apply for a business loan, applicants must complete the business training class that Four Bands offers. A great deal of technical assistance and training is provided before anyone may take out a loan.

The staff at Four Bands Community Fund takes a case-management approach to business-loan clients. Clients who wish to apply for a loan are asked to fill out a self-assessment form. Then a loan officer works with the client to identify areas of strength and weakness and develop a personalized technical assistance plan. Clients are provided with a range of technical assistance resources, including financial education and credit repair as well as training on how to write a business plan. The technical assistance is provided in workshop and one-on-one formats. Four Bands Community Fund offers quarterly "talking circle" meetings to discuss topics such as marketing, bookkeeping, and expanding profitability. Once a loan has been granted, follow-up technical assistance is provided. Four Bands Community Fund requires quarterly financial statements to be submitted to the loan officer, a policy implemented after learning from the Fund's work in the field that there was a lack of bookkeeping and finance skills

among a lot of small-business owners. The staff uses this loan require-
ment as an opportunity to provide ongoing technical assistance to help
their clients develop an internal accounting system, look at budget
to actual, and determine their cash flow. Clients are required to meet
quarterly with the loan officer, and at that time are provided with one-
on-one counseling and made aware of other training programs in the
community that may be of interest. Four Bands Community Fund also
provides intensive professional coaching for any client who requests it.
Even the credit-builder loans have action plans associated with them.
Clients create action plans for what they are going to do to manage
their finances and maintain and build good credit.

Training Programs

In addition to their loan products, Four Bands Community Fund offers
a range of training programs. It offers a comprehensive business development class called "CREATE" that helps people start businesses in a
remote, rural, reservation-based community ("CREATE" is an acro-
nym for "Cheyenne River Entrepreneurial Assistance Training and
Education"). In addition, Four Bands offers several financial-education
courses every year, and an IDA program designed to help people learn
the savings habit and build assets. Recently they have started a program to help introduce youth to entrepreneurship and help them develop financial literacy skills. In addition to their classes and programs,
they also offer one-on-one technical assistance to help people successfully manage and grow their businesses. As mentioned earlier, the
technical assistance includes coaching on marketing, financial and
staff management, and action planning. Recently, Four Bands began
working with other community leaders to start a Chamber of Commerce for community members. In addition, they worked with the
tribe to develop new business ordinances, and developed a joint filing
agreement with the state of South Dakota.

Impact

Four Bands is a small organization with an annual budget of approximately $600,000 per year. But its impact is significant. In the first eight
years of operation, Four Bands provided training programs to 1,531
people. It has graduated 169 people from its business classes, and provided a range of technical assistance and training services to over 575

adults and 325 youth. In addition, Four Bands has contributed over $76,358 in savings match for their IDA program participants. Since 2000, it has approved over 121 loans totaling approximately $669,000. Its default rate is 12 percent of the total funds deployed, and includes several microloans and two larger loans amounting to about $60,000 made to businesses that failed. The failure of one of the larger business loans was due to a problem related to a lack of legal infrastructure on the reservation. The tribal court ruled against a business owner who had a legal partnership agreement. When his partner pulled out and took a large share of the assets, the owner was not able to litigate successfully in the local tribal court system. Another business had a problem with employee theft that made it difficult for the business to turn a profit. The other loans failed because of the low capacity (lack of business acumen) of the borrowers.

Four Bands Community Fund is working to reduce this default rate, and they always try to work out any problems with a borrower and negotiate new conditions if necessary. Successful businesses assisted by Four Bands increased their annual incomes by anywhere from $6,000 to $26,000 and created an average of 1.5 jobs per loan, and include a successful plumbing and heating business on the reservation and several smaller home-based businesses. Another successful business they supported is a company that makes collapsible storage units for the Department of Defense and employs twenty-six people on the reservation. In the past seven years, Four Bands Community Fund has supported or assisted over seventy businesses on the reservation. The economic impact of these investments is much larger after the local multiplier effect is taken into account.

Lessons Learned

The executive director of Four Bands Community Fund, Tanya Fiddler, cites several key lessons learned about running a loan fund on a reservation. One key challenge can be developing the market for loan products. Fiddler (2008) stated:

> You create the capacity in that customer over time which takes a lot longer for you to grow the capacity of the loan fund for any potential earned income opportunity . . . Lakota Fund [another Native CDFI] is finding the same thing. They increased their

staff to 16 people in the last year, and their loan volume did not increase. It is a capacity issue out in the community. You really have to have a strong strategy for growing that capacity. With financial education—you start making people aware—this is the real deal.

Fiddler (2008) identified the challenging economic environment as a key barrier to economic development:

We are creating economies here. Everyone knows that people leave the rez, the money leaves the rez . . . you have to market twice as hard to get people to buy locally. The largest employers are the tribe, the school system, the IHS, all institutional employers. We are working hard to build the private sector.

Four Bands Community Fund has found it difficult to generate enough income to support operations without aid from outside donors. For example, because of their remote, rural location and the fact that they have fewer revenue streams, they have trouble meeting the self-sufficiency ratio recommended by the CDFI Fund. Fiddler (2008) suggested that

the self sufficiency measure should have a Native adjustment. We work as hard as we can to meet that, but we are only at 6 percent. But the depth of what the community needs on the development service side, it is capacity building—and those training programs end up consuming the operations just to get the capacity to get people through the doors to access a decent amount of money.

Four Bands Community Fund is improving the financial infrastructure in its reservation community by providing access to different credit products as well as business assistance and financial education. They have also contributed to the social infrastructure in the community by provided financial education to a broad range of adults and youth, with the expectation of creating the next generation of borrowers and role models in the local community. The work of Four Bands has contributed to asset building by providing loans to help people start and grow small businesses, and alternative financial products to help people clean up their credit and avoid predatory lenders.

Citizen Potawatomi Community Development Corporation

CPCDC is a not-for-profit loan fund program of the CPN, a federally recognized tribe in Oklahoma. Founded in 2003, its mission is to "to promote, educate, and inspire the entrepreneurial growth and financial well being of the CPN tribal community through financial education, access to capital, business development services and innovative capacity building practices" (Citizen Potawatomi Nation 2008). CPCDC's services focus on the provision of microloans and small-business loans to tribal members nationwide and Native Americans throughout Oklahoma, and also on providing personal loans to employees of the CPN. It is a small organization with a $500,000 annual budget, and was certified by the CDFI Fund in 2004. The CPN is headquartered in the town of Shawnee, which is approximately thirty-six miles from Norman Oklahoma and forty-eight miles from Oklahoma City. The population of Shawnee, Oklahoma is 29,989, and 18 percent of individuals live in poverty. In Pottawatomie County, Oklahoma, where Shawnee is located, over 11 percent of the population is Native American, 15 percent of individuals live below the poverty level, and 17 percent of all Native American families with children under the age of eighteen live in poverty.

The CPN is the largest of the eight federally recognized Potawatomi tribes, and the ninth largest tribe in the United States. The CPN has 26,000 tribal members living across the United States, with approximately 40 percent (10,400) of tribal members in Oklahoma, where its primary office is located. Most tribes in Oklahoma do not have reservations, but instead have traditional territory in Oklahoma Tribal Statistical Areas.

History

CPCDC was planned and founded as part of a multistage economic-development strategy designed by the tribal government to provide capital and technical assistance for projects that help to create a healthy tribal economy. The tribe has long recognized that creating access to capital for businesses and aspiring entrepreneurs will help its members achieve self-sufficiency. In addition to its collaborative relationship with the tribe, CPCDC fulfills a unique role as the only Native CDFI serving all Native Americans in Oklahoma as well as Citizen Potawatomi tribal members throughout the United States, and has been very successful in providing small-business loans and technical assistance to its target market.

When the tribe created CPCDC, they created a separate tribal affiliate corporation to run the loan fund. That corporation then applied to the Internal Revenue Service for a letter verifying their status under section 7871 of the Internal Revenue Code, which verifies that they are able to receive tax-deductible donations. The tribal government has been very supportive of its tribal affiliate corporation, and has invested almost $1.4 million in CPCDC. The organization has leveraged that support and has developed an extensive capitalization strategy, seeking to diversify its funding by looking to banks, foundations, government sources, individuals, religious institutions, and other institutional investors.

Financial Products

CPCDC offers a range of loan products and training programs. Since its inception, the organization has offered two main lending programs: the Micro Business Loan Program (loans up to $25,000) and the Commercial Loan Program (loans up to $200,000). The commercial loan product can be used for purchase of equipment, inventory, supplies, or working capital. It is also applicable to commercial real estate acquisition and refurbishment. These loan products are different from others offered in the community, because CPCDC conducts a more lenient credit analysis than most banks and at times requires less collateral.

CPCDC provides ongoing technical assistance to loan clients, which they believe increases the probability of success for the businesses they invest in. Staff provides loan applicants and interested individuals with an initial consultation to identify needs and specific areas of interest, and then prepares a customized action plan, recommending workshops and counseling as appropriate. Through one-on-one consultation and workshop instruction, participants learn how to prepare a business plan, obtain financing, set up a bookkeeping system, conduct market research, prepare effective advertising, handle contracts with government entities (tribal, federal, and state), and understand legal issues. A business plan is required before a loan is granted. After the loan is closed, staff continues to provide ongoing support to borrowers through one-on-one counseling and also through a range of classes and workshops (see the sections that follow). Recently, staff has also begun to provide customized management through the use of QuickBooks, as they have found—through site visits and in monitoring loan clients—that many loan clients need assistance with basic bookkeeping and financial management.

In 2005, CPCDC began offering a new loan program to employees of the CPN. The CPN Employee Loan Program makes small loans (ranging from $500 to $1,500) to tribal employees and provides financial education, including one-on-one counseling, monthly workshops, and credit counseling. Tribal employees make payments on their loans through payroll deduction, and they are given up to two years to pay off the loan. This loan program has helped reduce wage garnishments and has provided funds for people to deal with emergencies. The tribal government was very supportive of this program and provided $250,000 to capitalize the loan pool. Both the tribal government and the employees view this program as an employee benefit, and it provides an alternative to payday lending operations. There has been tremendous demand for this program: in the first two years, the program made 834 loans totaling over $664,000 (all funded by the original $250,000 invested by the tribe). This loan product has generated more than $100,000 in program income.

Training Programs

To complement its lending programs and to support the success of its lending clients, CPCDC offers a range of training programs. These include business training programs, general financial education, an IDA program, and free tax-preparation services.

Business Training

CPCDC's business training programs support its primary mission by strengthening the skills and knowledge of existing and potential borrowers and by supporting IDA savers who have identified entrepreneurship as a goal. CPCDC staff and leadership believe that consistent support safeguards the viability of projects, contributes significantly to the success of the business, and keeps loan losses low. Training programs play a special role in helping low and moderate-income Native American borrowers improve their financial and business-management skills and understand credit instruments. The goals of the business training program are to safeguard loan fund investment through the provision of training and technical assistance and to strengthen Native American businesses through ongoing, preloan and postloan technical assistance. Business training programs are offered through group workshops and one-on-one technical training. In 2007, CPCDC provided more than 1,144 hours of business development and training or consulting to Native Americans in Oklahoma and Kansas. This included 140 hours of direct, one-on-one consultation to Native Americans in the CPN regional area, with the remainder offered in small-group settings.

Financial Education and Related Training Programs

CPCDC offers financial education in a range of formats. CPCDC staff provides workshops and one-on-one counseling. Workshops are scheduled monthly and one-on-one credit counseling is scheduled weekly, according to referrals and on an as-needed basis in conjunction with other program participation (such as the IDA program). CPCDC staff uses the culturally relevant curricula "Building Native Communities— Financial Skills for Families" (developed by First Nations Development Institute and the Fannie Mae Foundation), "Money in Motion" (developed by the American Center for Credit Education), and "Credit When Credit is Due" (created by Credit Consumer Credit Counseling Service of the Black Hills).

A series of "Lunch and Learn" programs are provided for tribal employees, where people can receive information about budgeting, using credit wisely, credit repair, identity theft, retirement savings, and other topics. CPCDC also has a booth at the annual powwow and other events to share information about financial topics. The CDFI works in partnership with other tribal government departments—the Indian Child Welfare Department helps battered women learn financial skills, and the Housing Department incorporates financial education into its home-ownership training. The tribal government is very supportive of these efforts, and the Tribal Human Resources Department provides funding to pay for food at the "Lunch and Learn" workshops.

In a parallel effort, CPCDC has supported a Volunteer Income Tax Assistance (VITA) site every year to help people access the Earned Income Tax Credit (EITC), which can equal over $4,000 for a family of four. Many people had been accessing the EITC through predatory tax preparers, and had been losing up to 40 percent of their tax return to hidden fees. The CPCDC VITA site offers free tax preparation, thus keeping more money in the local economy. The number of participants in this program has grown each year. More recently, staff at CPCDC has been encouraging people to leverage their EITC windfall by opening an IDA account.

CPCDC started an IDA program in 2006 after attending a CDFI Fund-sponsored training on IDAs. The IDA program, which is called an "Asset Builders Matched Savings Program," offers small-business development and credit repair as savings goals. Applicants must be over the age of eighteen and enrolled members of a federally recognized Indian tribe (preference is given to members of the CPN). They also must live in Pottawatomie County or one of its five contiguous counties. Participants are required to attend credit counseling and financial-education classes and save a minimum amount of money each month to receive the match. As of October 2007, twenty-three people had graduated from the program and had received over 672 credit-repair training hours and 434 business-development training hours. The fifteen credit-repair participants saved over $11,510, and received a match of $21,000. An additional $30,736 of debt was paid off by credit-repair participants during the program time frame. The eight business participants saved $6,815 and received a match of $14,530.

Impact

CPCDC is unique in that it has just implemented a detailed tracking program to better measure program services and program outcomes. It has collected data in the past on jobs created and businesses assisted. It is now trying to collect more detailed outcome data on the percent of applicants that are low-income borrowers, the average wages of jobs created, and even the increase in individual clients' income as a result of their programs. This information will assist in better measuring CPCDC's economic-development outcomes in the community.

The basic data CPCDC has collected over the past seven years tells an impressive story. As of 2007, CPCDC's business-loan programs had made over 107 loans totaling over $6.9 million. One hundred percent of these loans have been made to Native Americans, 90 percent of whom are members of the CPN. The default rate on their loans is 1 percent, a low rate that CPCDC attributes to the effectiveness of its technical assistance to borrowers. The reach of its loan program is truly national: eighty-seven loans were made in Oklahoma, but eight were made in Kansas; four in Oregon; two each in Mississippi, California, and Missouri; and one each in Kentucky, Montana, and Texas. CPCDC provided over 1,144 hours of business-development training and 886 hours of financial education, in addition to the hours provided in its IDA program. The loans have contributed to the creation or retention of over 111 jobs. CPCDC has also matched over $35,000 for its twenty-three IDA program participants in the first year of its IDA program, amounting to a total impact of $85,011 when the participant's savings and additional debt payments are figured in. The IDA program helped participants create or expand eight new businesses and create ten new jobs. As already stated, its employee loan program has made 834 loans totaling over $664,000, most likely diverting much of this money from the portfolios of predatory lenders.

Lessons Learned

Some early lessons learned include the fact that "back-end TA," or continual technical assistance to loan recipients after the deal has closed, is as important as "front-end TA," or technical assistance before closing the loan. Cindy Logsdon, the loan officer we interviewed, spoke of the importance of staying in touch with loan clients to offer assistance and coaching. She stated, "We need to stay in contact, and the more assistance we can offer, the more successful they can be. It can be hard to provide that after the loan is closed, but it is very, very important." Another lesson learned is that IDA programs can really make a difference in people's lives. Cynthia stated, "It is one thing to pay down debt or start a business. But seeing people's self-confidence improve, seeing them succeed and their lives change, means so much more."

Conclusion

CPCDC addresses issues related to the financial infrastructure of their Native community by providing access to different credit products as well as business assistance and financial education. It is also addressing the challenges associated with the social and cultural infrastructure or their community by creating a new generation of Native American business owners and role models. Overall, CPCDC's work has contributed to asset building in the local community by providing loans to help people start small businesses and create jobs, and has helped limit asset stripping from predatory lenders by providing financial education and offering alternative financial products.

Lac Courte Oreilles Federal Credit Union

LCOFCU is a nationally chartered credit union located in Hayward, Wisconsin. Its mission is to provide basic financial services, consumer loans, and financial education to tribal members on the Lac Courte Oreilles Ojibwe Band of Lake Superior Chippewa Indian Reservation (LCO reservation). Hayward, Wisconsin is located adjacent to the LCO reservation. Over 23 percent of the population of Hayward is Native American, and the poverty rate in the community is approximately 13 percent for individuals. Sawyer County, which includes part of the reservation, has a poverty rate of approximately 12 percent. Little Round Lake, the most populous community on the reservation, has a Native American population of 900 (90 percent of the total population), and 42 percent of individuals live in poverty (American FactFinder 2008). Tribal population given by the U.S. Census was 2,886 in 2000. According to the Bureau of Indian Affairs, the unemployment rate in 2001 was 65 percent. The LCO reservation is very rural and is isolated from many markets and services. The closest city is St. Paul, Minnesota, which is 139 miles away. Green Bay and Madison, both in Wisconsin, are over 275 miles away.

History

LCOFCU was created because many tribal members living on the reservation did not have access to basic financial services like savings accounts. The housing authority did the initial market research, using a one-page survey that was distributed to clients. The research, funded by the tribal housing authority through a federal housing grant, demonstrated that there was a great need for financial products such as low-interest consumer loans as well as training programs such as basic financial-education training.

A community group presented the idea of a credit union to the tribal council in 1999. The tribe recognized the need for a local financial institution that was designed specifically to serve tribal members and expressed its support by signing off on the federal charter application. One of the main supporters of the credit union was the comptroller for the tribe in 1999 and is now the chief finance officer for the tribe. LCOFCU was legally created in 2001, when its national charter was approved, and is now a Native-American-managed 501(c)(4) federal credit union. It is also a CDFI that was certified by the CDFI Fund in 2002. "We always knew we needed to be a CDFI," stated David Fleming, the former president. "We knew that the financial education was key—not just the loan products." LCOFCU currently has over 1,700 members, and the tribe is a major source of deposits for the credit union.

Financial Products

LCOFCU offers a range of financial products and training programs to the residents of the LCO reservation and members and employees of the LCO tribe. In contrast to the other CDFIs we have profiled, LCOFCU is a depository institution and provides savings accounts and certificates of deposit.

LCOFCU also offers several credit products, many of them designed to provide an alternative to predatory lending. LCOFCU offers several basic consumer loans for new and used autos and other consumer purchases. Clients must undergo a credit check and are required to provide some collateral, although the credit union requires less collateral that most other lenders in the area. LCOFCU works with borrowers to help them understand the terms of the loan and receive credit counseling and financial education when necessary. People receive a lower rate on their loan if they have completed a financial-education course. The staff at LCOFCU employs a more lenient credit analysis than many lenders. David Fleming (2008), the former executive director of the LCOFCU, stated:

Our used car loans were a lifeline for some people. We required less collateral than most people, and in some cases allowed 100 percent financing. We took chances on people, and usually they paid off. People told us that being able to buy a car helped them keep their job. We allowed them to get into a car when everyone else was saying no.

Another credit product, called "Easy Money," is for tribal employees who have been on the job for at least one year and work at least thirty-two hours a week. This allows clients to borrow up to $500 without a credit check, and the money is paid back through payroll deduction. Designed to be an alternative to predatory lending, this loan program is very popular. The credit union has worked with the tribe to secure loans with payroll deduction so that individuals can get access to credit at reasonable rates. Two other smaller loan programs are part of the Easy Money program and are called the "Santa Loan" program (officially, the "Save our Santa" program) and the "Summer Loan" program (officially, the "Save our Summer" program). These programs allow people to take out seasonal, short-term consumer loans, and they have the same guidelines as the Easy Money loan products. The default rate on these short-term loans is lower than on the consumer loans, which staff attributes to the use of payroll deduction.

A third credit product is called a "GOOD" loan, which stands for "Getting Out Of Debt." This loan is designed to help people clean up their credit so they can qualify for a larger consumer loan. To qualify for a GOOD loan, which is given in increments of $500, clients must complete a financial-education course and then use the loan to pay off the debts that appear on their credit report. LCOFCU reports the repayment progress to the credit bureau, helping people repair their credit and build their credit score.

The average loan at LCOFCU is just $600, well below the minimum that other local financial institutions are willing to lend. But these small loans have a big impact. "The idea is that we do a simple, low-cost loan so our people won't have to go to a pawn shop or a payday lender or a check-cashing store," stated David Fleming. "If they keep coming in our door, we keep exposing them to more and more financial education, and, hopefully, we start to keep more wealth in our own community." LCOFCU staff reports that the major competition for such credit is a business on the reservation called "Payday Loans," which charges very high annual interest. One of the missions of LCOFCU is to provide an alternative to predatory lending to reservation residents, and to stop that form of asset stripping in the local community. In 2006, over 22 percent of LCOFCU's total loan portfolio was in antipredatory loans.

Training Programs
LCOFCU also offers several training programs, including financial-education classes, credit counseling, and credit repair. LCOFCU works closely with the Lac Courte Oreilles Ojibwe Community College to offer a standalone financial-education course at least four times a year, and to provide free tax-preparation services through a VITA site that is open during tax season. LCOFCU is currently preparing to develop an IDA program, and has also considered offering classes in investor education. LCOFCU also offers financial education and credit counseling to all its borrowers. "People would come in and not realize that a loan was not what they needed," stated David Fleming. "What they really needed was to check their spending habits. We would work with them and try to get them on track."

Impact
The LCOFCU is a small organization with an annual organizational budget of approximately $400,000. As mentioned above, they have over 1,700 members, and the tribe is a major source of deposits for the credit union. They have over $1,270,940 in active loans and $410,185 in deposits. Their delinquency rate on loans is 6 percent.

Lessons Learned
Staff at the credit union have identified several lessons learned. One of the most significant lessons was the need to work with the community to provide financial education and to "build customers." Echoing the lesson learned by Four Bands Community Fund, staff at LCOFCU identified the fact that few community members had the skills needed to take out a loan. "We didn't have a lot of borrowers in the beginning. We needed to make our borrowers. We needed to cover some basic information with applicants—explain to them their income-to-debt ratio, things like that," said Fleming. The financial education and credit

counseling was an important part of the CDFI's work. Some of the barriers were psychological: many of the borrowers had never used a bank before. David Fleming (2008) stated:

> Our goal is not to make a lot of money, but to establish a healthy relationship with that borrower. Instead of going to [a] pawn shop or payday lender, they come to us. We want to build relationships with borrowers. The goal of the credit union is to provide an alternative, getting people to come in the door. We hope they are learning to trust banks. Many have never been in a bank before.

Staff at LCOFCU worked closely with borrowers when necessary. David Fleming (2008) said,

> When someone lost their job at the tribe, or couldn't pay their loan, we wanted them to be comfortable coming to talk with us. We would work with them to refinance, or lower the payments on the loan until they got back on their feet. This made a difference and helped people learn to trust us.

Another lesson learned is that the "low-stakes" loans were important stepping-stones to becoming creditworthy. The smaller credit loans, including the Easy Money loans, allowed people to learn to use credit responsibly. The payroll deduction ensured that people had a low default rate. David Fleming (2008) stated:

> Many people told us that the "Easy Money" loan made them creditworthy—gave them a credit history, or helped improve their credit score. We reported payment on those loans to the credit agency and it helped people establish or repair credit. People told us that it made them eligible for a home loan later on.

Conclusion

LCOFCU is improving the financial infrastructure of the local community by providing access to loans and other financial services. But LCOFCU is also addressing social and cultural issues by helping to change attitudes about money and credit in the community. In addition to the direct efforts at building community knowledge and skills in financial management and providing better alternatives to high-interest predatory lenders, LCOFCU has, like most credit unions, provided a sense of belonging and ownership for the credit-union membership, especially for tribal members. LCOFCU president David Fleming states that the biggest impact he has seen from the credit union is "changing financial habits. People are actually seeing the benefits of savings in creation of their own individual wealth, and by becoming more money conscious and understanding how money and credit work."

Lessons Learned

Each of the three organizations profiled in this article is finding ways to provide access to credit in their local economies and promote asset-building in support of economic development. The case studies yield several lessons learned.

There Is a Need to Grow a Market for Credit Products in Native Communities

One lesson learned was the need to build demand for credit products in high-poverty Native communities. Interviewees emphasized the need to "grow customers" and "grow your market" for loan products, and pointed out that expanding the pool of funds available for lending did not automatically lead to higher loan volume in many high-poverty areas. Key informants at all of the case-study sites believed they needed to provide financial education and credit repair to a majority of clients to help them become creditworthy before they could even take out a loan, something that they learned through their market studies and ongoing work with customers. All three of the sites provide unique credit products (often called "starter loans") to help people learn to use credit responsibly (or in some cases repair credit) before they go on to taking out a larger loan (two of the CDFI managers we interviewed emphasized the need to build capacity in borrowers so that they can go on to take out larger loans). Our interviewees discussed the increased costs associated with providing intensive technical assistance and smaller loans that do not provide much revenue, and one key informant suggested that high-poverty rural and Native communities may need to adjust their expectations regarding self-sufficiency and income related to loan volume. The need to develop or cultivate a market for credit products may be true of other high-poverty communities in the United States, and this question should be explored in future research on the CDFI field.

A "Case-Management" Approach to Clients

Another lesson learned is the need to provide intensive, ongoing technical assistance to loan clients. Termed the "case-management" model by one of our interviewees, this approach to supporting clients seems to be particularly important in some Native communities where there are few experienced borrowers or business owners. Leaders at Four Bands Community Fund, LCOFCU, and CPCDC discussed the need to work with clients before, during, and after the loan closing to identify areas of need and to offer clients technical assistance, training, and consulting. This "high-touch" approach allowed the CDFIs to provide training in key areas such as bookkeeping skills, which market studies revealed were lacking in many borrowers. In addition, this approach allows for building capacity in borrowers so they are less likely to default on a loan. Four Bands Community Fund develops personalized technical-assistance plans for each borrower and requires quarterly meetings with its loan clients as a condition of closing the loan. It has found that these provide an opportunity to offer continual counseling, help with troubleshooting, and direct clients to training opportunities. CPCDC works with clients to develop a personalized action plan before offering a loan, a practice it believes has lowered the default rate on its loans.

Use of a Unique Credit Product to Build Financial Literacy, Increase Credit Scores, and Combat Predatory Lending

A third lesson learned is the need to use small loans to help people build or repair credit, avoid using predatory lenders, learn the process of paying back a loan, and become comfortable with working with banks. Four Bands Community Fund, CPCDC, and LCOFCU all offer loan products that are designed to help people learn to use credit responsibly and, in some cases, build or repair credit. CPCDC and LCOFCU both offer small consumer loans at a reasonable interest rate to provide an alternative to payday lenders, thus meeting the demand for small short-term consumer loans with an affordable product and redirecting some of the market demand from more usurious predatory loans. Each of the key informants we interviewed acknowledged that the revenue from these loans was minimal, but they emphasized the community development impact of helping people build or repair credit, avoid predatory lenders, and build their capacity as borrowers.

Ongoing Challenges

Although these Native CDFIs have been successful in providing access to capital to support small-business development and other asset-building programs, they continue to experience ongoing challenges. The first of these challenges is finding resources to carry out their work. Many of our key informants spoke of the difficultly of relying on their lending portfolio for an income stream and emphasized the need to raise funds from foundations and the federal government to carry out their work. CPCDC is fortunate to have the investment and significant financial support of the tribal government. LCOFCU manages several accounts for the tribal government, which provide it with a dependable revenue stream. But Four Bands Community Fund is almost entirely dependent on federal and foundation funds, and even the other two CDFIs continually draw upon outside resources to continue their programs. This raises questions about sustainability and whether these CDFIs will be able to rely solely on their services to support their operating ongoing expenses. A second challenge is the fact that in high-poverty areas, it can be difficult finding enough loan clients for a CDFI. As mentioned above, two of the CDFIs found that they had to carefully cultivate their markets for financial services. The CDFIs that do make loans often struggle to lower default rates. This suggests that few CDFIs serving high-poverty Native communities will be able to go to scale very quickly. A third and final challenge is the need to build the skills of borrowers, specifically the financial-management and bookkeeping skills of small-business owners. Through their market surveys, loan management, and business classes, staff at all three of the CDFIs identified poor financial-management skills as a challenge to successful business lending in their diverse Native communities.

Conclusion

CDFIs offer a locally controlled, community-responsive resource for credit and other financial services to support asset-based development in Native communities. Our case-study research provides examples of the ways that Native CDFIs can provide access to credit, training, and small-business development in support of asset building and community economic development. Beyond providing financial services, CDFIs can contribute to the social infrastructure in Native communities in support of asset building and economic development by creating role models, providing youth education, and developing a mentor class of successful business owners.

Native CDFIs play a unique role in addressing the problem of underdeveloped Native and reservation economies by providing the capital, training, and technical assistance necessary to support the Native-owned businesses that have begun to redirect ownership and control back into the Native communities. The importance of Native CDFIs in addressing this challenge cannot be underestimated because many future Native entrepreneurs are interacting with credit for the first time. Native CDFIs—by providing access to financial services, training and technical assistance, and role models for entrepreneurship development—are a critical part of developing an enabling environment for economic development in Indian reservations and other Native communities.

Notes

1. A portion of the land on Indian reservations is held in trust for Indian people by the federal government. Because of the legal status of the land, it is difficult to use trust land for collateral because banks have no ability to foreclose on the loan.

2. Uniform Commercial Codes (UCCs) provide a legal framework for economic transactions on Indian reservations as well as common legal definitions for the terms used in lending. Banks and other financial institutions are

more likely to conduct business on Indian reservations that have a UCC in place (see Clement 2005).

References

Adamson, Rebecca, Sherry Salway Black, and Sarah Dewees. 2003. *Asset Building in Native Communities*. Fredericksburg, VA: First Nations Development Institute.

American FactFinder. 2008. Retrieved August 20, 2009. http://factfinder .census.gov/home/saff/main.html?_lang=en

Boshara, R. 2001. *The Rationale for Assets, Asset-Building Policies, and IDAs for the Poor*, in *Building Assets: A Report on the Asset Development and IDA Field*. Washington, DC: Corporation for Enterprise Development.

Carr, Patrick. 2006. *Native Community Development Financial Institutions: A CDFI Coalition Analysis of Native Program Participation in CDFI Fund Programs*. Arlington, VA: CDFI Coalition.

Citizen Potawatomi Nation. 2008. *Citizen Potawatomi Community Development Corporation*. Shawnee, OK. Retrieved on March 20, 2008. www .potawatomi.org/Services/Small+Business+Loan+Program/Main/default .aspx.

Clement, Douglas. 2005. "A model law: A newly drafted model law may help bring loans to Indian Country." *Fedgazette* (March). Minneapolis, MN: Federal Reserve Bank of Minneapolis.

Community Development Financial Institutions Fund. 2001. *The Report of the Native American Lending Study*. Washington, DC: U.S. Department of the Treasury, Community Development Financial Institutions Fund.

Cornell, Stephen, and Joseph Kalt. 1997. *What Can Tribes Do? Strategies and Institutions in American Indian Economic Development*. Los Angeles: University of California, American Indian Studies Center.

Dewees, Sarah 2004a. *Family Economic Success in Native Communities: Adapting the Annie E. Casey Family Economic Success Framework to Rural and Reservation-Based Native Communities*. Fredericksburg, VA: First Nations Development Institute.

———. 2004b. *Investing in Community: Community Development Financial Institutions in Native Communities*. Kyle, SD: First Nations Oweesta Corporation.

———. 2004c. *Research Report: An Evaluation of the Impact of the Theodore R. and Vivian M. Johnson Scholarship Foundations' Investment in Entrepreneurship Education in Ten Native Communities*. Fredericksburg, VA: First Nations Development Institute.

Dewees, Sarah, and Lou Florio. 2003. *Sovereign Individuals, Sovereign Nations: Promising Practices for IDA Programs in Indian Country*. Fredericksburg, VA: First Nations Development Institute.

Dewees, Sarah, and Stewart Sarkozy-Banoczy. 2007. "Transforming economies: Entrepreneurship development in native communities." Pp. 155–191 in *Integrated Asset-Building Strategies for Reservation-Based Communities: A 27-Year Retrospective of First Nations Development Institute.* Longmont, CO: First Nations Development Institute.

———. 2009. *Investing in Native Community Change: Understanding the Role of Community Development Financial Institutions.* Rapid City, SD and Longmont, CO: Oweesta Corporation and First Nations Development Institute.

Edwards, Karen, and Aaron Schultz. 2007. "Financial management skills in native communities." Pp. 9–40 in *Integrated Asset-Building Strategies for Reservation-Based Communities: A 27-Year Retrospective of First Nations Development Institute.* Longmont, CO: First Nations Development Institute.

Egan-McKenna, Gene, and Susan Gabriel. 1991. *Conducting Reservation Economic Impact Studies: A Manual for Tribal Planners and Decision Makers.* Falmouth, VA: First Nations Financial Project (now First Nations Development Institute).

Fiddler, Tanya. 2008. Personal interview, conducted April 1.

Fleming, David. 2008. Personal interview, conducted April 4.

Flora, Cornelia, and Jan Flora. 1993. "Entrepreneurial social infrastructure: A necessary ingredient." *ANNALS of the American Academy of Political and Social Science* 529:48–58.

Flora, Jan, Jeff Sharp, Cornelia Flora, and Bonnie Newton. 1997. "Entrepreneurial social infrastructure and locally initiated economic development in the nonmetropolitan United States." *Sociological Quarterly* 38: 623–645.

Ford Foundation. N.d. *Building Assets to Reduce Poverty and Injustice.* New York: Ford Foundation.

Four Bands Community Fund. 2005. *Four Bands Community Fund 2005 Annual Report.* Eagle Butte, SD: Four Bands Community Fund. Retrieved on March 14, 2008. www.fourbands.org/annual.htm.

———. 2007. "About ss." Eagle Butte, SD: Four Bands Community Fund. Retrieved August 15, 2007. www.fourbands.org/about.html.

Hertel, A.L., K. Wagner, J. Phillips, K. Edwards, and J. Hale 2008. *Dialogues on Assets in Native Communities: Recording a Native Perspective on the Definition and Benefits of Retaining and Building Assets.* St. Louis, MO: Washington University, Center for Social Development and Buder Center for American Indian Studies.

Hicks, Sarah, Karen Edwards, Mary-Kate Dennis, and Christy Finsel. 2005. *Asset Building in Tribal Communities: Generating Native Discussion and Practical Approaches.* Center for Social Development Policy Report 05-19. St. Louis, MO: Washington University, Center for Social Development.

Hillabrant, Walter, Judy Earp, Mack Rhoades, and Nancy Pindus. 2004. *Overcoming Challenges to Business and Economic Development in Indian Country* (MPR Reference No. 8550-931). Princeton, NJ: Mathematic Policy Research, Inc.

Jorgenson, Miriam, and Louis Mandell. 2007. *The Financial Literacy of Native American Youth.* Rapid City, SD: Native Financial Education Coalition.

Juare, Ruth. 2006. *Native American Credit Union Initiative Proceedings.* Retrieved on August 20, 2009. http://www.ncuf.coop/media/Native%20American%20Convening%20Proceedings%20White%20Paper%20Final.doc

King, Juliet, Sarah Hicks, Karen Edwards, and Alisa Larson. 2003. *American Indian Tribal Communities and Individual Development Account (IDA) Policy.* Center for Social Development Policy Report. St. Louis, MO: Washington University, Center for Social Development.

Lui, Meizhu, Barbara Robles, Betsy Leondar-Wright, Rose Brewer, and Rebecca Adamson. 2006. *The Color of Wealth: The Story Behind the U.S. Racial Wealth Divide.* New York: The New Press.

Malkin, Jennifer. 2003. *Financial Education in Native Communities: A Briefing Paper.* Washington, DC: First Nations Development Institute, Corporation for Enterprise Development, and the National Congress of American Indians.

———. 2004. *Native Entrepreneurship: Challenges and Opportunities for Rural Communities.* Washington, DC: Corporation for Enterprise Development and the Northwest Area Foundation.

Malkin, Jennifer, and Jonathan Aseron. 2006a. *Native Entrepreneurship Nationwide and in South Dakota: A Summary Report to the Northwest Area Foundation.* St. Paul, MN: Northwest Area Foundation.

———. 2006b. *Native Entrepreneurship in South Dakota: A Deeper Look.* St. Paul, MN: Northwest Area Foundation.

Meeks, Elsie. 2006. "Entrepreneurship on tribal lands." *Economic Development America* 4:21–23.

Miller, Robert. 2001. "Economic development in Indian Country: Will capitalism or socialism succeed?" *Oregon Law Review* 80:757–859.

Northwest Area Foundation. 2008. "Highlights for Dewey County" and "Highlights for Ziebach County." St. Paul, MN: Northwest Area Foundation. Retrieved on August 1, 2008. http://www.indicators.nwaf.org/DrawRegion.aspx?RegionID=46137.

Schneider, Bettina, Stewart Sarkozy-Banoczy, Michael Roberts, and Sarah Dewees. 2007. "A Catalyst for Asset Building: Native Community Development Financial Institutions." Pp. 127–154 in *Integrated Asset-Building Strategies for Reservation-Based Communities: A 27-Year Retrospective of First Nations Development Institute.* Longmont, CO: First Nations Development Institute.

Sherraden, Margaret Sherrard, Cynthia Sanders, and Michael Sherraden. 2003. *Kitchen Capitalism*. Albany: State University of New York Press.

Sherraden, Michael. 1991. *Assets and the Poor: A New American Welfare Policy*. New York: M.E. Sharpe.

———. 2003. "From the Social Welfare State to the Social Investment State." *Shelterforce Online* (no. 128 March/April 2003). Retrieved on September 12, 2006. http://www.nhi.org/online/issues/128/socialinvest.html.

Smith, Kyle. 2003. *Predatory Lending in Native American Communities*. Fredericksburg, VA: First Nations Development Institute.

Tiller, Veronica E. Velarde. 2005. *Tiller's Guide to Indian Country: Economic Profiles of American Indian Reservations*. Albuquerque, NM: BowArrow Publishing Company.

Yin, Robert. 2002. *Case Study Research: Design and Method*, 3rd Edition. New York: Sage Publications.

3 Asset-Based Community Development in Alabama's Black Belt

Seven Strategies for Building a Diverse Community Movement

EMILY BLEJWAS

Introduction

In a global economy, rural communities must pursue new economic strategies to remain viable. Many communities are choosing strategies that build on inherent community assets instead of seeking to recruit outside industries. This chapter documents one town's use of asset-based community development in Alabama's Black Belt. Examining the challenges and successes of the art movement in the town of York, Alabama allows a glimpse into how asset-based community development works and offers other communities concrete strategies for building diverse, cohesive movements.

The town of York—population 2,500—sits at the far west edge of Alabama's Black Belt, well over one hundred miles from the state's most populous cities of Birmingham, Montgomery, and Mobile. Like many rural American towns, York has experienced a decline in population, jobs, and resources in recent decades. York's young people pursue better opportunities elsewhere, industries continue to pass it by, and poverty rates soar. Once a booming railroad town and the hub of the county, York has seen its downtown shops close one by one, leaving the main street full of boarded-up stores and empty of people.

Many in York recognize the limitations of traditional economic strategies in a global economy that is based on technology and innovation. Residents have witnessed firsthand the departure of longtime manufacturers and the resulting loss of jobs and a stable economy. Many residents now believe that industry will not locate in York and that the town needs to build on what it already has. To this end, York residents have turned their focus toward creating a new economy by building on their assets: a pastoral setting, a twenty-five-year-old art center, downtown art galleries, and dedicated citizens.

To grow the movement, however, York residents must form a cohesive group, overcoming the racial segregation present since the town's inception. In York, Blacks and Whites attend separate churches, businesses, restaurants, and social clubs. When the federal desegregation ruling passed in 1969, Whites in York chose to construct a private academy instead of sending their children to integrated public schools. This segregation persists to this day, with almost all Blacks attending public schools and almost all Whites attending private academies.

Segregation has dire implications for community development efforts that hinge on mobilizing whole communities behind a cohesive movement. This chapter examines how the art movement in York has begun to bridge the racial divide and offers seven concrete strategies for fostering diverse and cohesive community movements. These strategies grew out of the experiences of a small Southern town, but can be implemented wherever community development is at work.

Asset-Based Community Development

In recent decades, rural areas have witnessed the centralization of agriculture, the downturn of manufacturing, and the rise of a global economy based on technology and innovation. These trends have caused rural areas to fall increasingly behind in wealth, job opportunities, health care, transportation facilities, school adequacy, infrastructure, and overall well-being (Willits and Luloff 1995). Rural areas are experiencing numerous problems, including persistent out-migration of youth, poverty, and lack of employment opportunities (Lewis 1998:102). Thus, rural communities must develop new strategies to promote economic and community success. Suzanne Wilson and colleagues (2001:132) state that "since the 1970's, economic restructuring and the farm crisis have reduced rural communities' economic opportunities, making older development strategies less viable and forcing many to look for nontraditional ways to sustain themselves."

Many rural communities are pursuing asset-based community development, touted by scholars and practitioners as an effective development method that encourages communities to recognize and reinforce assets within the community instead of relying solely on recruiting outside industries. Joe Sumners and Larry Lee (2004:28) explain that "successful communities 'think outside the box,' looking for ways to set themselves apart from the pack. They identify what makes their community special and then work to cultivate and promote those unique assets." The asset-based method strengthens both the community and its economy and helps to ensure development efforts will be sustainable (Medoff and Sklar 1994; Mubangizi 2003; Shuman 1998).

History of Art in York: 1981–2001

Twenty-five years ago, two local artists held a craft conference in a barn on their property, inviting community members to share and learn art. Tut Altman Riddick, a native of York with long family ties to the area, taught mask-making at the event. The sight of so many local citizens making art convinced Riddick of the need for an art center in York. Riddick's goal was to expose people in the Black Belt to contemporary art, but she believed an art center would benefit the York community in other ways as well. She sought to make a place for the artist, as there were few recreational outlets in York outside of hunting and football. She also viewed art as a bridge, capable of pulling people and communities together.

Riddick began asking local residents for property and donations for an art center in York. Some local residents doubted York could support anything like an art center because of the town's rural quality. Interestingly, many of those working to make the art center a reality also worked together in a campaign opposing a large hazardous-waste landfill owned and operated by Chemical Waste Management (Alley, Faupel, and Bailey 1995; Bailey and Faupel 1992). The experience of working together for a common cause provided these individuals with a background in community organizing that would benefit the art movement.

Riddick secured a vacant building, and the city of York donated tax revenues to renovate it and to employ a part-time director. A handful of prominent families also donated funds. The Coleman Center opened in 1985 and featured the Riddick art collection, but soon local residents expressed interest in showing their own art. The Riddick collection was relocated to the Mobile Museum of Art with the intention of bringing it back to fill in when needed at the Coleman Center, but that was never necessary. Local art sustained the Coleman Center for the next fifteen years, featuring the work of hundreds of local and regional artists. The Center also sponsored book signings, speakers, workshops and a yearly festival called Rooster Day.

At first, York residents viewed the Coleman Center shows without much comment. "People would come in and not say a lot, but just look," Riddick explains, "but we were excited about the response, that people came to the shows." Over time, however, Riddick believes the Center helped to develop an art sophistication among local residents. Visitors to the gallery began critiquing what they saw, and several citizens of York and its surrounding area who first encountered art at the Coleman Center later emerged as artists or art teachers.

However, Riddick downplays the amount of support she received for the Center. She maintains that it enjoyed little community support and that some residents supported it only because they had nothing else to support or because Riddick's family was popular in York. Riddick is also realistic about the amount of time it takes to cultivate an appreciation of the arts. She explains:

> For a lot of people, art is not a part of their early culture. You can't knock people for something they haven't grown accustomed to. Like, I have no need for a computer. Why should I take on something I don't need? Art is the same for some people. The principal at the public high school in York had never been to an art gallery or art store when we opened the Coleman Center. There is a difficulty in trying to communicate art in that context.

Some York residents, however, believe the Coleman Center benefited the community more than Riddick allows. Residents call it "amazing" and "remarkable" that a town so small and rural has supported an art center for over twenty years. A former fundraiser states:

> People from all over Sumter County stepped forward and made nice contributions because they were happy about the Coleman Center. It brought a sense of community throughout the county. The most amazing thing was how the Coleman Center brought people together I never thought would have come together for the purpose of supporting the arts, especially in an area of hunting and football. But even the hunters and football fans gave money and enjoyed the [events].

A New Phase of Art in York: 2001–2005

During its first fifteen years, the Coleman Center employed a series of part-time directors and focused on regional crafts and artists. At the turn of the century, however, art in York entered a new phase when two prominent artists came to live and work in the town. In December 2001, Marilyn Gordon came to York to direct Black Belt Designs, a sewing project intended to help local women recently laid off by closed textile mills to improve and market their sewing skills. In April 2002, Amos Kennedy came to York as an artist in residence. Kennedy is a well-known print artist whose reputation in the Southeast and connections in the art world helped attract other artists in residence to York.

Indeed, the presence of Gordon and Kennedy did wonders to promote York. The Coleman Center director at the time decided to raise funds to hire two new full-time directors to make use of this newfound talent and attention. Thus, in August 2003 a new executive director began reorganizing the board of directors, developing a mission statement, raising new revenue sources, and formulating a strategic plan and a Coleman Center Web site. The new artistic director began recruiting artists in residence to come to York and design a series of public art projects.

The artist-in-residence program was a major new addition to the art scene in York. Artists from outside of Alabama lived in York for a few weeks or months and were provided with housing and stipends for materials and living expenses. The artists were required to develop projects that actively engaged citizens in the creation of art, beautified York, and served a function. Projects included a bench at a youth bus stop, an audio collection of local music, a bicycle shed where youth could learn to repair bikes, and several sculptures based on York history.

The artist-in-residence program boosted both outside interest in York and community momentum for the arts. One York resident believes the new directors and artists in residence "brought the Coleman Center from being a local museum to a center doing things anyone from any large city would see as art. They raised the bar for all of us." The new directors departed York in the summer of 2005 but were replaced by directors who have continued the Center's focus on recruiting artists in residence and designing public art projects.

In January 2004, another major event boosted the art movement. Eight downtown buildings were auctioned to five local artists and two buyers who planned to open restaurants. The eighth building sold to the city of York, whose mayor still hopes to use it for an art-related purpose. The burgeoning art movement encouraged the buyers to purchase the downtown buildings. The general conclusion has been that the artists would not have bought the buildings without the Coleman Center as the driving force. Artists' purchase of the downtown buildings boosted the York art scene. In addition to the five artists working at the Coleman Center every day, there were now four glass artists, a music teacher, a sculptor, and a basket maker working in downtown York. The downtown artists who had previously worked independently in their homes now worked side by side on the main street of town, which enhanced their cohesion as a group and increased community interest in their work. The downtown artists also worked with the Coleman Center to keep the arts growing in York by directing visitors to the Center and collaborating on several community art projects.

Effects of the Art Movement

When the downtown artists moved into their studios in the summer of 2004, one artist brightened the sidewalk outside her shop with plants and flowers, which had a trickle-down effect on the block. Soon, all the artists had flowers out front, and many of the older stores added them as well. The same thing happened during the holiday season: one artist put up lights and every single store on the block followed. The flowers and lights gained a huge community response. (One artist even claims she heard more positive comments about the plants than about what she sells inside her studio). The downtown artists believe that the simple act of adding flowers and lights to the main street in town did wonders to increase civic pride in York.

These early, visible changes in York showed citizens that change was possible, built momentum, and established the art movement as active and credible. One York resident states that the energy "has spilled into the whole community and gotten everyone interested. I never thought art could do that, but it has." Another agrees, "York has a spirit, an energy, things are picking up, people are excited about what's happening." A resident who grew up in West Alabama in the 1980s states that at that time "York was nothing, it was a gas station, a stop on the way to Tuscaloosa. But now there's something going on, something York needed for a long time."

New energy in York has inspired new projects, including plans for a sports complex and the renovation of a local park. The York Beautification Board reorganized and held a contest for the best-looking lawn. Two local residents renovated a corner downtown building and installed a blues café. The Coleman Center hired Auburn University's Small Town Design Initiative to conduct community-planning sessions to produce a plan for York's revitalization. In these sessions, York citizens catalogued assets: York's location as a gateway to Alabama, proximity to two freeways, railroad history, small-town character, and an art movement. The assets were then translated into a poster containing a plan for York's future.

Art in York continued to draw outside attention. Alabama Public Television visited over a dozen times to film a documentary, and *Southern Living* reporters also showed interest. Articles appeared in several local papers and in two Birmingham, Alabama newspapers. York also boosted outside attention by holding First Saturdays—community art days held the first Saturday of every month. Visitors came to walk York's streets and admire the public art, buy from the shops and studios, visit the Coleman Center gallery, and eat food sold at booths by local residents.

Perhaps the greatest validation any community can receive is to be regarded as a prototype by surrounding communities, a status York has achieved. The Black Belt Action Commission touts York as a model for other small communities. A publication by the Economic and Community Development Institute at Auburn University cites the York art movement as a prime example of a "diverse and innovative economic development strategy" for rural Alabama, describing York as a community "open to any opportunities that align with community assets . . . to new ideas and [to] new ways of doing things" (Sumners and Lee 2004:27–28).

York also inspired the development of Black Belt Treasures, a Web site and gallery in Camden, Alabama (eighty miles southeast of York) that sells Black Belt art. Its founder visited York because the art movement was reviving the town and giving residents a sense of pride and direction. Former Black Belt Treasures director Linda Vice (2005) states:

> We looked at York as an anchor. During our planning phase, we benefited from their long experience. We avoided people thinking you can't do it because we could point to York as an example. York just took what they had and made a product out of it. It's not a pretty town, it has no architecture or famous social movements, but they now have a national reputation. Their vision set the standard for the rest of us who wanted to improve cultural assets in the area. Black Belt Treasures is an outgrowth of what we saw in York.

Vision for York

York residents view art as an economic strategy, citing the recent rise and success of rural art tourism. Tourists are increasingly seeking rural getaways, especially those that offer an encounter with local or folk art. Some residents go beyond seeing York as a tourist destination and envision it as a center for art learning. Riddick hopes York will grow to resemble Penland, an art school in Spruce Pine, North Carolina.

York residents hope to achieve their vision by continuing to build on assets, including York's location, small-town feel, energy and momentum, and art and artists. Residents believe York needs to offer a tourism package, with the whole town made attractive and convenient to tourists. This requires improving the town aesthetically, beautifying the main street, offering lodging downtown, and increasing the number of restaurants. York residents also cite the need for marketing, publicity, and creating partnerships with other organizations.

According to some residents, however, the most critical need for the York art movement is broader community support. These residents recognize art as an excellent opportunity to reverse York's decline but know it will succeed only if the whole community is motivated. To gain broader support, however, the art movement must overcome the high degree of racial segregation present in York since its inception. As Sumners and Lee (2004:21) state, "Economic progress requires the resources of the 'whole' community. Communities that are divided— racially, politically, or socially—face near-insurmountable barriers to economic advancement."

Segregation in York

Longstanding segregation in York has caused the formation of two separate cultures. Blacks represent 78 percent of York's population and often exist in a world separate from that of Whites. Blacks and Whites in York attend separate schools, businesses, churches, community groups, restaurants, clubs, and are even set apart in some area cemeteries that contain fences dividing White graves from Black. As one resident states, "York is fractured socially by race issues."

This custom of separation is perhaps perpetuated most strongly by segregated schools. When the federal government demanded the desegregation of Alabama schools in 1969, White York residents maintained segregation by constructing private academies. White families who could not afford to attend were either sponsored by wealthier community members or left town. To this day, virtually all Black students in York attend public schools while all White students attend private academies, public schools in other counties, or are home schooled. Many in York believe school segregation is the main reason the town remains so racially separate. One resident defines segregated schools as "the biggest challenge facing York because children in York grow up without an opportunity to mix with people who are different from them."

Segregation in York yields several effects that hinder community development. Segregation divides limited resources and fuels a heightened awareness of race. In fact, a visiting artist in residence who had conducted community art projects outside of the South was surprised when White students in York drew themselves with a yellow marker, even though the paper was white. "They were really aware of the color of their skin," he states, adding:

> There is a heightened awareness of race in York which causes some things that are not about race to get pushed into being about race when the issue is really more personality driven. It's easy for things to fall into the race category, and it gets to the point where there's so much tension around race, how could things not be about it? It precedes everything.

Segregation also incites distrust and stereotypes, thwarting communication between the Black and White communities. It prevents Blacks and Whites from developing friendships with one another, which are necessary for the mutual trust and common work that precede community development. York residents explain that it is difficult to step outside social mores to break down racial barriers, citing "the invisible line" or "the old community convention" that keeps Blacks and Whites in their respective places.

Segregation in the Art Movement

Segregation in York seeped into the art movement, often blocking attempts to create a cohesive community movement. In York, many spaces are viewed as Black or White and the Coleman Center was no exception. Despite its founders' conception of it as a neutral institution, the Coleman Center developed a White identity. York residents have referred to it as "a White institution" and as "something that Blacks do not do." The point is perhaps best illustrated by an anecdote from a local White artist who offered a Black York resident a tour of her studio in the Coleman Center in 2003. He responded, "Can Black people go in there?"

Because it was viewed as an establishment for the White elite, the Coleman Center initially attracted and involved a narrow group of participants. Most of its donors were wealthy Whites. It once held an opera event to raise money, and one of its two yearly fundraisers was a wine and cocktail party. In fact, to form the Coleman Center's fundraising body in 1991, leaders obtained the membership list from the all-White Sumter County Fine Arts Council and invited its members to a meeting. At the very first meeting, officers were elected and dues were paid, making it impossible for anyone outside of the Sumter County Fine Arts Council to be an elected officer of the Friends of the Coleman Center.

Segregation has fueled perceptions of racism within the art movement. One incident occurred when a White woman rather than a Black man was hired in 2005 as the new Coleman Center director. One Black York resident believed the Coleman Center did not want a Black person in charge. This hiring decision may or may not have been racially motivated; the more important point is that members of the Black community perceived racism while members of the White community did not. In a town as segregated as York, the incident reflects a vicious cycle that is caused and perpetuated by the lack of trust between the Black and White communities.

An anecdote from a Black business owner illuminates the lack of trust and communication between the Black and White communities and how it stifles development. The business owner states that some White members of the art community brought photographs of one of his buildings to the city council and asked that it be condemned because they believed its appearance was a detriment to York. He states:

> The art community is not approaching it right. If they want me to beautify my buildings, why not offer me grants? Or why not ask me? Say, 'As soon as you are able, why don't you do something about it?' I care about beautiful things. I never dream of streams with milk cartons and foam in them, I dream of streams with clear running water, water pure enough to drink. They need to find a way to help instead of finding fault. I had hard times for three or four years, and after this, it looked like they just wanted to keep it hard instead of helping.

Seven Strategies for Building a Racially Integrated Movement

A York artist in residence states that "in small towns, there is a lack of cooperation between people that is needed to create the institutions and practices that make a town grow. It's the same for York. For the town to grow in the arts, it has to grow in so many other ways. It has to change the way it sees itself as a town." Many York residents would agree. Indeed, although York is a long way from achieving racial integration, residents stay the course because they believe Blacks and Whites must work together for the art movement, and for the community as a whole, to succeed.

Although integration is a slow process, the art movement has experienced some success in unifying Blacks and Whites. The Coleman Center has become a rare place in York where Black and White can interact. It has brought different segments of society together and diversity to area arts. Importantly, the strategies used to unite Blacks and Whites in York can be applied in any community seeking to unite disparate groups behind a cohesive community movement.

Create a Neutral Space

Many York residents believe racial segregation is maintained not out of hostility, but out of habit and a lack of opportunity for social exchange. Even youth of different races do not interact in York, as there is no forum in which to do so. To create such a forum, leaders in York's art movement took deliberate steps to make the Coleman Center a neutral community space. Directors recognized the ability of the Coleman Center to serve as a unifying force in the community and sought to establish the Center as a place welcoming to all races.

Make Effective Contact

Because Blacks did not initially view the art movement as open to them, movement leaders knew they must reach out to the Black community to increase participation. It is not enough to simply declare the art movement as open to all. Rather, its leaders must make deliberate and effective contact with the Black community. A recent

North Carolina study found that among residents who did not attend community meetings, "a staggering 81 percent" did not participate simply because they did not know about the meeting (Laurian 2004:59). Thus, community leaders can increase Black participation in the arts by effectively contacting and communicating with the Black community.

To do this, York leaders have gone into the community instead of requiring the community to come to them. When the Coleman Center opened in 1985, Riddick printed five hundred invitations and went to every post office in Sumter County to hand them out personally. As a result, five hundred people attended the opening. Riddick also created Rooster Day, a yearly art festival held in downtown York. In addition, local artists have gone into local schools and created projects in downtown York. Thus, instead of requiring residents to come to the gallery to see art, the Coleman Center installed art on community billboards, benches, sidewalks, and in a local park. "The art got out in front of people," states one resident.

Art movement leaders could further increase Black participation by extending personal invitations to Black community leaders. Some York residents believe that if the Coleman Center were to extend personal invitations to Black organizations, Black participation would be enhanced. Church leaders are a particularly powerful force in rural Alabama. Thus, if art movement leaders can gain the support of church leaders, the church leaders could convince their parishioners of the art movement's worth and boost local support for it.

Design Community Projects

To increase community participation in the arts, Coleman Center directors have designed community projects. For example, the Community Memory Map consisted of two large maps of York that residents filled in with memories, photographs, drawings, stories, and poems. Likewise, artist in residence Stuart Hyatt listened to live music in York for four weeks, then wrote eight songs inspired by what he had heard and recorded eighty-eight people in the community singing them. A former Coleman Center director explains that this was the first time a lot of York citizens had been in the same room together. She calls it a

"Sumter County harmony moment," adding that the most eye-opening and moving part of her experience at the Center was when artists in residence conducted projects that engaged the community.

By creating opportunities for Blacks and Whites to interact and work together, community projects increase the interracial friendship and trust needed for community development to succeed. Sumners (2005:14) points out that, in the Black Belt community of Uniontown, Alabama (fifty miles east of York), as Blacks and Whites focus on the interests they have in common through community development efforts, "the differences between them begin to seem smaller. . . . Relationships are being established across the issue of race, not by dealing with the issue explicitly or talking about racial barriers or how to overcome them. Rather, trust is developing as Black and White citizens work together on projects to bring about community improvements." Likewise in York, simply working together on Coleman Center projects has brought Blacks and Whites together.

Target Youth

Many in York believe the path to integration is through the schools. One of the strongest powers of art in York is its ability to provide opportunities for building interracial relationships among youth who have no other forum in which to do so. Movement leaders hope that after seeing an integrated art program, residents will begin to envision and pursue other ways to integrate youth in York, thus moving closer to integrating the schools.

Youth programming also increases community participation in the arts by drawing in adults. When the Coleman Center conducts projects in schools, the parents of participating students begin to attend Coleman Center events. Several York residents believe that if the art program can get children involved, their parents will come to cheer them on, giving the art movement the family and community support it needs. Indeed, York residents cite youth projects as a major reason the Black community has begun to participate in the art movement.

The Coleman Center's *Your Art Here* project, for example, gave fifth and sixth graders at public and private schools an opportunity to make drawings about their community. The drawings were then collaged, enlarged, and featured in the Coleman Center gallery and on three billboards around town. The Coleman Center director believes residents connected to *Your Art Here* because they had a personal tie to it. At the opening, several people made comments like "My grandson did that" or "I know someone who goes to school there." Adults were willing to approach art movement leaders because their children had already gotten to know them through the project.

Recruit Minority Experts

Asset-based community development relies on local experts who know local resources and can garner the trust, respect, and participation of the community. Choosing who delivers the message of community revitalization is critical. Leaders should be highly respected in and knowledgeable about the community. They should have a connection to a broad base of local citizens and an ability to bring them to the table. Without these local experts, there is no way to gain local buy-in or to create a sustained development effort.

Local experts have boosted participation in York's art movement in several ways. First, the Coleman Center has featured the work of local Black artists. In fact, a poetry reading by a Black York resident drew more members of the Black community to the Coleman Center than ever before. The poet believes that if the Coleman Center were to more aggressively recruit Black artists to exhibit their work at the Center, it would draw more people to participate, and their families and friends would come to support them.

Black participation also increased with the arrival of Amos Kennedy, a Black artist in residence. Kennedy is credited with attracting diverse participants to the Coleman Center and helping to change its identity into one of racial neutrality. One York artist believes that because Kennedy is Black, he has helped Blacks feel welcome in the art movement and has increased dialogue and understanding between Blacks and Whites. Indeed, one Black resident states that he knows of the Coleman Center only because he is a friend of Kennedy.

The mayor of York has also championed the art movement and was key to pulling in the Black community. As a Black leader, the mayor strives to change the perception of the Coleman Center as a White institution. She has encouraged the Black community to attend Coleman Center events and claims "the more they attended, the more they became excited about art in York and talked about promoting it." She believes the Black community now "knows they are welcome at the Center and feels a part of it."

Coleman Center directors have increased the number of Blacks on the board of directors. Under new leadership, the board has increased in size, and the racial makeup is beginning to be more reflective of the community. By the summer of 2006, the board consisted of six Blacks, four Whites, and one Native American. Further, Blacks now occupy higher positions on the board than previously.

Be Relevant

Community development practitioners know that to involve average citizens, programs must be relevant. If citizens do not see how efforts affect them or those closest to them, they will not get involved. Thus, leaders must seek community input to design programs reflective of community desires and needs. Vaughn Grisham and Bob Gurwitt (1999:30) explain that leaders must "convince people it would be in their own interest to get involved. . . . People connect with community development when they understand how it affects them and their families." Citizens must also feel ownership over efforts. Grisham and Gurwitt add that "even the best ideas are impotent if they are not connected to, informed, and 'owned' by a larger body of participants" (1999:31).

Some York residents believe the art movement could increase its relevancy by giving the Black community a chance to direct programming. They believe the Coleman Center should get input from the public about what kinds of programs the community wants. In the past, Coleman Center monthly newsletters offered a space for citizens to express their preferences in programming. It may benefit the Center to reinstate this option, as well as to hold periodic community meetings.

The art movement could also increase Black participation by featuring various types of art of interest to the community. One artist in residence points out that music is a major folk tradition in West

Alabama and that performance poetry has deep roots in recitation traditions occurring in Black churches. Thus, he believes music and poetry programming would attract the Black community to the Coleman Center. In fact, he attributes the high attendance at a poetry reading not only to the fact that the *poet* was Black, but to the fact that *poetry* has strong Black roots.

Indeed, when members of Arts Revive in Selma, Alabama (eighty miles east of York) sponsored a program based on the experiences of Black quilters in Gee's Bend, Alabama, the response from the Black community was overwhelming. Black churches and Black sororities bought blocks of tickets. Arts Revive leaders believe the play was so successful because people could connect to it. Cofounder Molly Gamble states, "The play was of regional interest for everyone. Blacks and Whites" (Gamble 2007).

Choose a Unifying Method

"The thing that struck me about York," states an Alabama resident, "the bigger story, was that in a town in the Black Belt, which is 78 percent Black, this was the first time Blacks had socialized with Whites. Art crossed social lines in ways other activities hadn't in decades. I wondered, 'What is it about art that makes it a bridge?'"

York residents provide several responses to this question. They cite the accessibility of art, pointing out that because no one owns art, everyone can approach it. They cite the universality of art: people like art and music regardless of race. And they cite art's inherent neutrality. As Riddick states, "You can talk about quilts, pottery, or printing without getting people's back up."

Art can also provide a visual model of racial integration. By including White students from the private academy and Black students from public schools, *Your Art Here* blended the students' drawings to create a racially integrated vision of York. Some York artists also make art that is intentionally about embracing the larger community and breaking down "invisible barriers" and "color lines."

Thus, art in York can provide residents with new visions and ideas. Because artists show others a different way to see the world, their vision can broaden viewers' horizons. A former Coleman Center director offers a summarizing statement:

From school on into adulthood, most of the population [in York] remains segregated. Of course, it is not a forced segregation—it is a choice, and mostly people choose that way because they have never been given any other options. This is where I think the arts can play a role in helping with the race issue. Bringing artists into the community who are somewhat "alien" immediately presents someone who is totally different than what the norm is in York. And I think artists, in the end, "make things" that are somehow telling of our world—so giving the citizens of York the opportunity to view works by these artists also gives them new ideas and hopefully, new choices.

Conclusion

In the town of York, Alabama, Blacks and Whites remain separate in many facets of life, including churches and schools. Yet many York residents desire an integrated existence and believe Blacks and Whites would come together if given the opportunity. Further, many believe Blacks and Whites *must* come together for the art movement, and the community as a whole, to thrive. Thus, perhaps the art movement's greatest contribution to York is its provision of both a neutral space and a common goal to unite two disparate groups and lay the groundwork for future collaboration.

The art movement is not without its challenges. In recent years, some residents have expressed the opinion that the Coleman Center has strayed from its mission of showcasing local talent by focusing on artists from outside the region. Artists-in-residence Gordon and Kennedy, who helped spark a new phase of art in York, have both departed. The movement continues to struggle to gain local interest and support.

Despite these current struggles, however, the art movement has experienced some success in breaking down racial barriers in York. Importantly, this was accomplished through building on and redefining assets already in place: the Coleman Center, downtown artists, and a pastoral setting. It was accomplished through establishing a neutral space and common work to encourage and allow Blacks and Whites to come together.

This essay offers other communities a chance to benefit from York's success by learning how residents have promoted an integrated, cohesive movement. For asset-based community development to succeed, leaders must secure broad participation. Doing so is a challenge in divided communities like York, yet York residents have progressed in chipping away at racial barriers by deliberately seeking a broad set of participants. By utilizing the seven strategies presented here, other communities can work to overcome divisions and build diverse community movements.

Note

Research reported in this chapter was funded by a grant from the Alabama Agricultural Land Grant Alliance, the Alabama Agricultural Experiment Station, and the Alabama Cooperative Extension System.

References

Alley, Kelly D., Charles E. Faupel, and Conner Bailey. 1995. "The historical transformation of a grassroots environmental group." *Human Organization* 54:410–416.

Bailey, Conner, and Charles E. Faupel. 1992. "Movers and shakers and PCB takers: Hazardous waste and community power." *Sociological Spectrum* 13:89–115.

Gamble, Molly. 2007. Phone interview. August 22.

Grisham, Vaughn, and Bob Gurwitt. 1999. *Hand in Hand: Community and Economic Development in Tupelo.* Aspen, CO: The Aspen Institute.

Laurian, Lucie. 2004. "Public participation in environmental decision making: Findings from communities facing toxic waste cleanup." *Journal of the American Planning Association* 70:53–65.

Lewis, James B. 1998. "The development of rural tourism." *Parks & Recreation* 33:99–108.

Medoff, Peter, and Holly Sklar. 1994. *Streets of Hope: The Fall and Rise of an Urban Neighborhood.* Boston, MA: South End Press.

Mubangizi, Betty Claire. 2003. "Drawing on social capital for community economic development: Insights from a South African rural community." *Journal of the Community Development Society* 38:140–150.

Shuman, Michael H. 1998. *Going Local.* New York: The Free Press.

Sumners, Joe A. 2005. *Building Community: The Uniontown Story.* Auburn, AL: Economic Development Institute.

Sumners, Joe, and Larry Lee. 2004. *Crossroads and Connections: Strategies for Rural Alabama*. Auburn, AL: Economic Development Institute.

Vice, Linda. 2005. Personal interview. Camden, AL. November 22.

Willits, Fern K., and A. E. Luloff. 1995. "Urban residents' views of rurality and contacts with rural places." *Rural Sociology* 60:454–466.

Wilson, Suzanne, Daniel R. Fesenmaier, Julie Fesenmaier, and John C. Van Es. 2001. "Factors for success in rural development." *Journal of Travel Research* 40:132–138.

4 The Politics of Protected Areas

Environmental Capital and Community Conflict in Guatemala

MICHAEL L. DOUGHERTY
AND ROCÍO PERALTA

Introduction

In San Cristóbal Verapaz, Guatemala, peasant groups sought to improve sanitation infrastructure in order to mitigate the degradation of a local lake without limiting access to the environmental services that the lake provided to poor households. Local elites appropriated this process by converting it into an initiative to declare the lake and its watershed a protected area. These local elites, in cooperation with functionaries and politicians at the national level, sought to use the declaration of the area as protected to further their political aims. The findings of a group of consultants, hired by the local elites to plan the technical process of protected-area declaration, ended up supporting the peasant perspective—that a protected area was not in the interests of local development. These community conflicts eventually led to the abandonment of the initiative altogether.

Over the past fifteen years a new literature has emerged around the idea of building community assets to promote development and fortify rural communities against the adverse effects of the world market and commercial growth. Developing assets shores up community autonomy in the face of challenges from global capital (Shuman 1998). This asset-based community development (ABCD) framework has become popular among community development practitioners and academics, and in the United States, where it has been most widely applied, it has largely proven effective. This chapter looks at one kind of community asset, environmental capital, and applies this concept to rural Guatemala.

Because theoretical and empirical work on this development model is primarily focused on the United States, the documented successes of the asset-based development model often take place in the context of relatively effective local democracy characterized by strong institutions and minimal external influence. Institutional weakness and corruption characterize many political environments across the developing world. This chapter seeks to answer two research questions: Does the theoretical model of environmental capital hold up when applied to a developing country context, and what is the relationship of political institutional weakness to environmental capital-based development? The answer to these questions lies in the unique confluence of political institutional weakness and the multifunctionality of the natural landscape (Klein and Wolf 2007). The interaction of these phenomena can generate community conflict and stalemate rather than promote substantive development.

By applying the concept of asset-based development to the context of a developing world, this case study complicates the uncritical way environmental capital is commonly thought of. The community development literature employs a narrow definition of environmental capital that limits the relevance for the model outside of the United States and Western Europe. Ultimately, this study finds that elements of the natural landscape, commonly understood as "environmental capital" in the community development literature or "natural amenities" in the rural sociological and applied economic literature, fulfill different roles for different social groups—hence it is "multifunctional." An environmental asset is not a thing in itself, but a way of understanding a thing. With this in mind, this chapter develops a typology of ways of conceptualizing natural resources—the capital lens, the service lens, and the symbolic lens. We find that the capital lens—that is, the viewing of natural resources as tradable commodities—may be more appropriate in affluent economies characterized by relatively strong political institutions. In the developing world, other lenses that can stymie efforts to apply the asset-based development model may emerge.

This chapter contains six sections. The first section summarizes the asset-based development literature and briefly lays out the study's methodology. The second section provides a brief overview of the study site, its demographic composition, and its development indicators. The third, fourth, and fifth sections constitute the empirical substance of this article, the case narrative. In the third section we describe the community-based origins of the initiative to rehabilitate the lake, the formalization of the process by elite-led organizations, and the origins of social conflict in San Cristóbal. The fourth section describes the arrival of the consulting firm and the results of the technical study of the proposed protected area. Section five concludes the case narrative by describing the political fallout of the conflict in San Cristóbal. Finally, section six returns to the theoretical discussion and advances a new theoretical wrinkle in the literature on asset-based development.

Environmental Capital and the Global South

In 1993, John Kretzmann and John McKnight introduced the concept of ABCD as an alternative to the orthodoxy of the day—the needs assessment. They argued that focusing on the needs of the community rather than on its strengths, gifts, and talents had created cultures of frustration, nihilism, and dependence in marginalized areas. The alternative was to focus on residents' assets as a point of departure in planning for development. Kretzmann and McKnight defined assets as "individuals, associations, and institutions" (Kretzmann and McKnight 1993:6). They encouraged community development practitioners to find the gifts, skills, and capacities within, and between, community residents. Their ideas revolutionized academic literature on community development. But their limited definition of asset allowed the creation of social and human capital over the introduction of financial capital, which has limited the approach's resonance among some practitioners and politicians. Another approach to ABCD that was being developed around the same time—the community capitals framework—overcomes this potential limiting factor of Kretzmann and McKnight's approach. The community capitals framework is a way of organizing and conceptualizing Kretzmann and McKnight's assets that assigns them quantifiable economic values as well as moral value.

Throughout the 1980s, sociologists James Coleman (1988) and Pierre Bourdieu (1986) were developing concepts of nonfinancial forms of capital such as social, human, and cultural capital. Cornelia B. Flora and Jan L. Flora (2008) drew on these concepts and consolidated them into the community capitals framework for community development. The community capitals framework includes six forms of capital: financial, human, social, built, cultural, and natural capitals. Like financial capital, each of these forms of community capital can be invested to produce returns (economic or otherwise) to the investing community without depleting the principal. Human capital, for example, refers to the educational levels, training, skills, and aptitudes of community residents. By investing in education, individuals increase their earning power, which increases the amount of financial capital in circulation within a community. Social capital refers to the financial advantages of increasing the number and density of relationships between individuals and associations both within and beyond the community. These relationships produce additional economic capital because they assist in finding jobs (Granovetter 1974; Green, Tigges, and Browne 1995). They also create informal social networks that can buttress communities in times of economic stress and fortify democratic practice (Putnam 1993). Built capital, a community's physical infrastructure and housing stock, is key in assisting potential investors in making siting decisions and influences the choices of potential migrants into the community, thus shaping the introduction of financial capital into the area. Cultural capital aids community development by encouraging visitors to move to the community in cases where unique cultural attributes are promoted for tourism (Green and Haines 2007). Another definition, more closely related to human capital, holds that certain social classes are culturally more likely to generate higher returns from labor (Bourdieu 1986). Finally, the community capitals approach includes natural capital,[1] which is also referred to as environmental capital. Environmental capital includes the different ways in which natural resources like land, soil, and water can be used for community development. In sum, a few key texts have drawn from the theoretical work of Bourdieu, Coleman, and others and built upon the concepts of Kretzmann and McKnight (1993) to create the community capitals framework for community economic development (see Flora and Flora 2008 and Green and Haines 2007).

As with other forms of community capital, there is no one definitive understanding of environmental capital in the literature. The key community capitals literature acknowledges the multifunctionality of environmental capital and offers a distinction between the use values and the exchange values with which environmental capital is imbued. Karl Marx (1867), in developing his labor theory of value, distinguished between use value (value of a commodity determined by its level of utility to the human endeavor) and exchange value (value determined by the amount of another commodity it can be traded for in a market). Without using this specific terminology, Flora and Flora (2008:35) discuss the multifunctionality of natural capital. They describe seven types of values which natural capital possesses: provision, production, consumption, speculation, creation (as in the foundation for built capital), ecosystem services, and preservation. As this chapter will illustrate, this is not a comprehensive list of values. Environmental capital possesses amenity value (exchange value), direct consumptive value (use value), and symbolic value, which Flora and Flora do not discuss. M.B. Potschin and R.H. Haines-Young (2003) also develop a typology of functions of natural capital. They suggest that natural capital conforms to four types of functions—regulation functions, habitat functions, production functions, and information functions. Mary Ann Brocklesby and Eleanor Fisher (2003:195) also use the terms *use* and *exchange value* to refer to the community capitals approach. Also acknowledging the multifunctionality of environmental resources, Green and Haines (2007:169) categorize environmental capital as containing "direct use value" and "non-use value" although their definitions of these terms differ from the original Marxian definition of use value. Green and Haines' conceptualization of environmental capital does incorporate amenity value, but again misses symbolic value. The fact that symbolic value has been overlooked in the community capitals literature is not surprising. Symbolic value is a function of political institutional weakness characteristic of developing economies, yet the community capitals literature has been largely U.S.-focused.

The concept of environmental capital, although robust and useful in many respects, is imperfect and incomplete. Brocklesby and Fisher

(2003:195), for example, refer to the community capitals framework in general as "simplistic, lineal, and monothematic." They argue that reducing community assets to capitals results in "missing the human agency, practices, and social organization underpinning . . . community development." Jan Flora (1998:502), one of the architects of the community capitals framework, echoes Brocklesby and Fisher in writing that "the conversion of environmental capital to economic capital . . . resulted in deforestation, soil loss, and agricultural chemical usage." Jessica Crowe (2006) finds that high levels of natural capital are not significant promoters of self-development for rural communities in the American Northwest. Finally, Potschin and Haines-Young (2003) argue that unfettered exploitation of environmental capital poses ecological and human risks, and consumes these resources irreversibly.

In this chapter we use the Marxian distinction between use value and exchange value to frame our Guatemalan case study theoretically. By applying the notion of environmental capital to Guatemala, a country characterized by profound political institutional weakness, some of the limitations of the environmental capital concept come to light. In this chapter we suggest that environmental capital possesses three fundamental types of value: use value, exchange value, and symbolic value. Further, we argue that these values underpin the lenses through which environmental assets can be conceptualized in community development: the service lens, the capital lens, and the symbolic lens, respectively. Finally, we argue that these lenses cut along socioeconomic, and in this case, ethnic lines. Finally, we conclude that in the context of developing countries, the multifunctionality of environmental capital can generate community conflict, which can lead to degradation of community assets.

Although there has been robust debate around the asset-based development model for the United States and Western Europe, the framework has been sparsely applied outside of the developed world. This is ironic because the variations in political and economic environments between global north and south hold distinct sets of outcomes for asset-based development. The natural resources and comparative advantage of many parts of the developing world lend themselves to environmental capital-based strategies. Rural Guatemala, for example, offers abundant land and labor along with capital scarcity, which is an appropriate factor mix for a capital-unintensive, landscape-dependent development model. In capital-scarce economies that are rich in natural resources, environmental-capital-led development makes the most of comparative advantage while creating needed incentives for the protection and enhancement of natural resources. Additionally, asset-based approaches appeal to poor communities because they often require smaller capital investments than business recruitment models do. For these reasons, rural parts of some developing countries exploit asset-based development. Nevertheless, the political institutional endowments in these countries can be countervailing forces. This is the case because political institutions are generally weaker in capital-scarce economies. We use the term *political rents* to characterize the key manifestation of political institutional weakness in this case. In economics, a rent is a profit beyond what the market would establish. Rents are acquired through inappropriate market manipulation. The term *political rent* has been previously defined as "profits created politically" (McChesny 1987). Here *political rent* is used figuratively to refer to unearned or undeserved political capital extracted through antidemocratic forms of political entrepreneurialism.

This analysis is based on three sources of data: reports and documents of the protected-area declaration process, key-informant interviews, and participant observation. Grupo Sierra Madre (GSM), the Guatemala City-based environmental consulting firm that conducted the protected-area study, granted us access to all of their data. These data included focus group and interview transcripts, journal notes kept by the researchers, internal and external reports, and PowerPoint presentations designed for a range of stakeholders from community members to international funders. In addition, we traveled to San Cristóbal Verapaz in August 2006 and observed workshops conducted with community members on the topic of lake restoration. Finally, we conducted several open-ended, key-informant interviews with local elites, peasants, and external consultants during and after our stay in San Cristóbal.

The GSM data, on which this article is largely based, included open-ended interviews with community leaders and focus groups using Participatory Rural Appraisal methodology. The researchers sought community-based data that would both "complement and confront" their technical findings (Grupo Sierra Madre 2006:8). The focus groups were planned and organized during meetings between the consultants and community leaders in each community. The data-collection methods employed in the focus groups included a mapping exercise where participants were asked to draw accurate maps of their communities and then change the maps according to how they would like their communities to look in the future. Additionally, the research team recorded oral histories of the communities, with attention paid to environmental changes. These recordings were then transcribed and coded for analysis. The community-based research involved 309 focus-group participants and more than twenty key-informant interviews representing thirty different rural hamlets within the Chichoj watershed.

Development and Ecology in San Cristóbal Verapaz

San Cristóbal Verapaz is located in the southwest corner of the Department of Alta Verapaz in Guatemala's largely indigenous central highlands. The population of the municipality is 43,336, eighty-five percent of whom belong to the Maya-Poqomchi sociolinguistic group (Instituto Nacional de Estadística 2004).

Smallholder agriculture for national and international markets makes up 66 percent of the economy of San Cristóbal Verapaz. The second largest economic sector is manufacturing, at 10 percent. A national shoe company, Calzado Cobán, has its factory in San Cristóbal. The remainder of the economy consists of smallholder production for local consumption and services. Per-capita daily income is around U.S. $3.20 in agriculture and U.S. $5.13 in manufacturing. This is significantly below the national average (Grupo Sierra Madre 2006).

San Cristóbal ranks as the seventh most unequal municipality of Guatemala's 331 municipalities. Seventy-seven percent of the population lives in poverty and 30 percent in extreme poverty (Secretaría General de la Planificación 2002). Outside of the county seat there are virtually no municipal services provided. Most dwellings in the county seat are connected to municipal water and sewage, although the services do not function adequately (Grupo Sierra Madre 2006). The soil, forests, and aquifers from which the majority of local residents derive their livelihood have proved less resilient under the population pressures of the last few decades, and quality of life for many residents has slowly deteriorated.

The Laguna Chichoj is located on the edges of the county seat, effectively within the peri-urban area.[2] The Laguna forms the basin of the area's primary watershed. It collects runoff from communities in the surrounding mountains and in turn discharges into the Río Cahabón and eventually into the Caribbean Sea. The watershed, along with most of the municipality, is located in two ecoregions: encino pine forest and montane forest. This fact accounts for the watershed's importance as a central node along the migration trajectory of many endangered bird species and for its impressive diversity of local birds (Grupo Sierra Madre 2006:57). Also, the Laguna Chichoj has cultural significance for Guatemala as a whole and for the residents of San Cristóbal and the Poqomchi people, and it is a key contributor to the scenic value of the municipality (Grupo Sierra Madre 2006:35). Laguna Chichoj is considered one of Guatemala's thirteen national lakes and has a prominent place in the Guatemalan public consciousness. These unique aspects of the watershed make its conservation all the more urgent. Over the past four decades, as use of carcinogenic chemicals in daily life has outpaced public infrastructure to mitigate their effects on the environment, the Laguna Chichoj watershed has become highly contaminated and degraded. Given the growing problems of poverty, inequality, and environmental degradation, in 2003 a burgeoning peasant organization organized a campaign to save the Laguna.

The Origins of the Peasant Initiative in San Cristóbal Verapaz

The campaign to rehabilitate Laguna Chichoj had grassroots origins, although it was quickly appropriated by municipal elites and local political entrepreneurs. The campaign emerged from an initiative by a number of community development projects (Consejos Comunitarios de Desarrollo [COCODEs]). These COCODEs have their origins in national legislation. Decree 11-2002, Law of Urban and Rural Community Development Councils, was published as part of a package of decentralization laws that included a new municipal code and an administrative devolution law. In San Cristóbal, these COCODEs have been officially established in all of the rural hamlets and urban neighborhoods that comprise the municipality. Each COCODE is made up of a president, vice president, secretary, treasurer, and at least three additional executive members, and is registered with the Civil Registry of the Town Hall.

With the growth of democratic space at the community level in 2003, multiple COCODEs representing urban neighborhoods and rural hamlets in the Laguna Chichoj watershed began to recognize the importance of rehabilitating the Laguna. Despite its small stature and somewhat remote location, Laguna Chichoj is a national symbol. In addition to being one of Guatemala's thirteen national lakes, it was named in article 90 of the 1989 Law of Protected Areas as one of forty-four special protection areas. In decades past, Laguna Chichoj was a major tourist attraction and revenue generator for the local economy. Before contamination became so severe, swimming the length of the Laguna Chichoj was part of a well-known, internationally attended triathlon. Additionally, the lake, despite its severe degradation, continues to provide essential environmental services to the area's poorest inhabitants. The lake provides water for irrigation and washing, and some families still fish there. For these reasons, COCODE members reasoned that rehabilitation of the Laguna would be an important first step in any community revitalization plan. Furthermore, they reasoned, basic sanitary infrastructure had to be in place before meaningful environmental rehabilitation could take place because the Laguna is at the lowest point in the watershed and thus receives all of the runoff from agricultural byproducts and waste in the surrounding communities. To that end, this nascent, grassroots community network organized to lobby the municipal government for improved sanitation and water treatment services as well as potable water provision. This policy agenda coincided with community members' material goals of improved municipal services, and so the momentum behind the campaign grew. This initiative had two principal goals: (1) to rehabilitate the Laguna as a matter of public health and environmental service provision, and (2) to capitalize on the considerable environmental capital of the Laguna as a core component of a comprehensive community development plan.

Renewed attention to the Laguna and the diffusion among the population of the rhetoric of conservation and development eventually got the attention of members of the elite, educated stratum of San Cristobal's county seat. In the last few years two formal nonprofit organizations were established in the county seat: Asociación Verapaz (ASOVERAPAZ) and Grupo Asociado Salvemos al Lago (GASAL). ASOVERAPAZ formed in 2004 to undertake environmental education workshops for rural women whose lack of access to municipal water sources forced them to use the Laguna to wash clothing. GASAL's principal undertaking has been the removal of invasive species of aquatic plants that have proliferated in the nitrate-laden waters of the Laguna. These two organizations embraced the notion of saving the lake, but articulated policy goals that were at odds with the ambitions of the community development councils. For example, educating poor women about the environmental impacts of washing clothes in the Laguna does not address the core problem of lack of access to municipal services. Community members and outside observers questioned the local elites' commitment to their professed stewardship goals (Grupo Sierra Madre 2007). When ASOVERAPAZ and GASAL joined forces with the Town Hall to form the Environmental Roundtable for the Rescue of Laguna Chichoj in 2005, the rhetoric shifted from *rehabilitation* to *protection*. Consequently, the policy goals also shifted from improved municipal-service provision to declaring the lake a protected area under the National System of Protected Areas (República de Guatemala 1989). The COCODEs objected to this revised set of goals, arguing that because the hydrogeology of the watershed is such that the Laguna will always receive the runoff from surrounding communities, simply "roping off" the Laguna would not protect it from further degradation but would prevent communities from accessing the lake's environmental services. Although community members viewed the Laguna as a provider of ecosystem services, the local elites saw it as an opportunity to consolidate political power. An additional incentive for the Town Hall to appropriate the peasant-led initiative was the circumvention of responsibility for the expensive infrastructure projects that the peasant groups were calling for. The costs of protected-area declaration, in contrast, would not come from the municipal budget but would be absorbed by the National Council of Protected Areas (CONAP). Therefore, the rhetorical transition from rehabilitation to protection—with the establishment of the Environmental Roundtable—had symbolic as well as substantive meaning.

Local participants at the Environmental Roundtable included ASOVERAPAZ, GASAL, the mayor and other municipal functionaries, and representatives from COCODEs of three urban neighborhoods in the San Cristóbal county seat. Whereas COCODEs and their constituents had originally spearheaded the campaign, in this new incarnation their participation was marginalized. Other institutions with official representation in the Roundtable included the National Peace Fund (FONAPAZ), the Ministry of Environment and Natural Resources (MARN), and the Secretariat of Executive Coordination of the Presidency (SCEP). The creation of the Roundtable marked the beginning of coordination among the various institutions of civil society and local government. The Roundtable's initial activities included the creation of the Municipal Environmental Agenda, the coordination of efforts to extract invasive species of aquatic plants from the Laguna, and visits to Congress to discuss the possibility of declaring the Laguna a protected area.

The leadership of ASOVERAPAZ was creative and savvy. ASOVERAPAZ knew that the Laguna Chichoj had been listed in the 1989 Law of Protected Areas and intended to capitalize on that fact. They approached CONAP, which had recently entered into an agreement with the Netherlands Directorate General of Development Cooperation (DGIS) and the Tropical Agronomical Center for Research and Teaching (CATIE) of Costa Rica. DGIS, CATIE, and CONAP were collaborating on a project to conserve biodiversity and strengthen the bureaucratic and administrative processes for establishing protected areas in Guatemala. This trinational collaboration is hereafter referred to as the National Protected Area Management Project. ASOVERAPAZ's petition to CONAP dovetailed with the goals of the National Protected Area Management Project, and CONAP issued a call for proposals from consulting firms to conduct the technical study and operative plan for the declaration of Laguna Chichoj as a protected area. In May 2006, the Guatemala City-based environmental consulting firm GSM won the public call, and in June 2006 GSM began its research.

The Technical Study and Peasant Participation

The methodology for the technical study included a review of public documents on the municipality of San Cristóbal as well as species inventories, water-quality tests, analysis of soil types and usage, measurement of forest cover, and assessment of hydrology and geomorphology. Along with the technical data, the consultants conducted community focus groups and key-informant interviews to assess community support for the protected area. Community support—more than technical issues, they argued—would determine the viability of the project.

This research found that the priorities for rural communities were, first, water provision through the protection of natural springs and, second, waste-water management, reforestation, and appropriate farming techniques. Additionally, many community members pointed out natural attractions and scenic routes in their communities that they wished to develop into small-scale, amenity-based tourism attractions. All of the community concerns related back to quality of life and economic productivity rather than strict conservation and protection (Grupo Sierra Madre 2006:59).

The water quality studies showed that the Laguna could not maintain stable biotic communities and that the chemical and bacteriological composition of the water made it unfit for marine life and human consumption (Grupo Sierra Madre 2006). The technical study affirmed the COCODEs' arguments that population pressure within the boundaries of the watershed had increased at a greater rate than the capacity to provide an adequate infrastructure for health and sanitation, and until adequate systems of waste-water treatment and potable water provision were put into place, the recovery of the Laguna would not be feasible under Guatemala's Law of Protected Areas. After completing the technical study and before beginning the master plan, the consultants changed course. Rather than recommend the site be declared a protected area, they recommended it be declared a critical-management site. They drafted a plan for the critical-management site that would focus initially on expanding and improving municipal services, including potable water provision, waste management, and sewers (Grupo Sierra Madre 2006). This shifted the emphasis of the endeavor away from protection and back to rehabilitation.

The technical processes of rehabilitation and environmental management are not accounted for in the legislation concerning protected areas. Therefore, the responsibility of a critical-management site falls to MARN and not CONAP. Article Fourteen of the statute regarding the Law of Protected Areas (República de Guatemala 1989) states that CONAP has the jurisdiction to oversee recovery plans for areas that have already been established as protected, but there is no legal attribution for the technical processes of recovery for areas that have not already been declared protected. If Laguna Chichoj were to become a critical-management site rather than a protected area, CONAP would lose its authority over the site and the associated political rents. In such a scenario, management would fall to a new commission made up of local technicians approved by MARN and representatives from a variety of national institutions including MARN, the National Forest Institute (INAB), and CONAP (Grupo Sierra Madre 2007). The legal basis for the critical management plan and the establishment of a local management authority draws from the new Municipal Code and Decentralization Law (Decrees 12 and 14-2002) as well as from the new Health Code.

The consultants presented their findings and recommendations to the Roundtable. This created cracks in the veneer of consensus that Roundtable leaders had constructed. The COCODEs, which had been primarily concerned with improving municipal sewer and water service, saw the critical management plan as reflecting their material interests to a greater extent than the protected-area proposal. The Roundtable leadership, for whom protected-area status was a symbolic victory with significant political rent potential, ardently questioned the study's findings and categorically rejected its recommendations.

The GSM consulting team was made up of highly educated residents of Guatemala City of *mestizo* descent. The technicians ostensibly shared fewer cultural attributes with the peasants who constituted COCODE membership than local elites did. Therefore, it is ironic but telling that the external consultants and COCODE representatives found common ground in dissention from the policy agenda of the local elites. The consultants' community-based research confirmed that the COCODE's identified goals did, in fact, correspond with the material interests of the majority of peasants. Furthermore, the technical study of ecosystem integrity legitimized the arguments that CO-CODE members had made three years prior, furthering the case for the value of local knowledge and underscoring the importance of beneficiary participation in the development process.

The Political Consequences of the Technical Study

The character of the relationship among the consultants, the COCODEs, and the Environmental Roundtable began to change in September 2006 when the top three functionaries of CONAP left their posts for undisclosed reasons. The first to depart was the executive secretary. Her departure was followed by the director of the National Protected Area Management Project, and shortly thereafter by the deputy secretary (CONAP's second-highest ranking official). No official reasons were given for these high-level departures, although anonymous research informants speculate that the three were replaced by more politically amenable appointees.

Around the same time, evidence emerged of collusion between the political elites of San Cristóbal Verapaz and government functionaries at the national level. The former minister of the environment, who replaced the outgoing executive secretary of CONAP, reportedly demonstrated a feeling of personal entitlement to the Laguna Chichoj project, suggesting that there was political competition between CONAP and MARN for administrative authority of prominent amenity sites (Grupo Sierra Madre 2007). This kind of competition for political rents, between similar government ministries, is not unheard of. For example, in the United States there has long been competition between the Park Service and the Forest Service over how best to manage certain federal lands. Further pointing to collusion, the mayor of San Cristóbal had recently parted ways with his political party and realigned himself with the Gran Alianza Nacional (GANA), the party that held the presidency for the 2003–2007 term. The goal of this political maneuver was to enhance his potential for reelection by allying with the incumbent party. To cement the alliance between GANA and the mayor of San Cristóbal, Eduardo Gonzales, then the secretary of SCEP, came to San Cristóbal to stump for the mayor. Gonzales, at the time, was GANA's candidate for president in the 2007 elections.

Had they stayed on, the departed functionaries would have supported the technical study and its conclusion that making Laguna Chichoj a protected area was not feasible. In August 2006, before the technical study was rejected, GSM consultants presented their preliminary findings in the CONAP headquarters in Guatemala City. At the time of that meeting, CONAP's executive secretary had just left, but the deputy secretary and unit director had not yet departed. In that meeting, the then-deputy secretary and unit director of CONAP stated that they knew all along that Laguna Chichoj could not qualify as a protected area, but that they needed the study to confirm it. They described in detail the problems CONAP had faced in the similar case of Lake Atitlán, where a protected area was declared in a densely populated region. This shortsighted decision had imposed impossibly costly bureaucratic procedures on poor community members residing inside the protected area for a variety of banal aspects of daily life. For example, making slight modifications to a private dwelling within the protected area required an environmental-impact study authorized by CONAP, a significant bureaucratic imposition on peasant families (Grupo Sierra Madre 2007).

At this meeting, GSM and CONAP agreed to abandon the protected-area process and shift their attention to a rehabilitation plan for the Chichoj watershed that would not be bureaucratically burdensome for community members and would be more likely to achieve the development goals articulated by peasant groups in the area. The director of the National Protected Area Management Project changed the Terms of Reference of the contract with GSM to reflect this shift in focus and sent the documentation off to the national office of CATIE for approval. Shortly thereafter, however, both the deputy director and the project director left their posts. With the change of authorities, the process began to break down quickly.

The new authorities at CONAP sided with the mayor and community elites from ASOVERAPAZ and rejected the technical study and critical management plan on the grounds that they were technically deficient. CONAP submitted a twelve-page condemnation of the study to GSM and demanded that the study be redone, effectively, without additional timeline or budgetary allowances, which was obviously impossible. This had the effect of disrupting the community-based process of creating an organizational structure to implement the critical management plan.

The legal parameters of protected-area recovery in Guatemala are vague, which heightened the political tensions of this case. Because 2007 was an election year and technocrats at all levels are political appointees in Guatemala, CONAP may have refused to accept the conclusions of the technical study because doing so would have meant relinquishing oversight authority of Laguna Chichoj to MARN and losing the political momentum behind declaring the Laguna a protected area.

The technical team was made up of expert geologists, biologists, environmental scientists, and planners, so it was easy to interpret CONAP's rejection of the technical study as a political maneuver masquerading as a technical critique. GSM submitted the critique of their study to colleagues at two Guatemalan universities, who independently confirmed that the scientific basis for CONAP's rejection was spurious. Furthermore, because the proposed critical-management plan was drawn from the extensive community data collected in interviews and focus groups, and was supported by the COCODEs participating in the Roundtable, rejecting the plan was tantamount to rejecting the desires of the majority of citizens of San Cristóbal Verapaz.

Assets, Multifunctionality, and Political Rents

In Guatemala, civil society tends to view local government with a lack of trust. Because of the enduring legacy of government corruption, relationships between civil society and local government are often hostile and occasionally violent. In 2002, for example, citizens rioted in Tecpán, Chimaltenango when the mayor tried to implement collection processes for the nationally mandated, but locally administered, property tax. The police station and the mayor's home and car were burned, the town hall was vandalized, and an assassination attempt was made against the mayor (Palmer 2007). Another similar case took place in Aguacatán, Huehuetenango in 2003 when the ethnically divisive mayor, Pablo Escobar Méndez, was reelected with only 19 percent of the popular vote. A coalition of opposition parties and civilian supporters violently occupied the town hall, setting off two years of physical confrontations resulting in three deaths and assassination attempts against the mayor and his wife (Méndez 2007). This destructive tension is primarily a product of civil society's mistrust of local governments. Matthew Bond (2003:21), for example, writes that communities "see [tax collection] as yet another form of corruption."

In San Cristóbal Verapaz, this same destructive tension between local elected officials and peasant civil society is at work. The Environmental Roundtable in San Cristóbal was ostensibly created as a way to bring diverse community perspectives on the fate of Laguna Chichoj together. Yet community elites used the Roundtable and the protected-area declaration process for political purposes that were incompatible with the desires of the peasant majority. Furthermore, the mayor of San Cristóbal presided over the Roundtable, and the Town Hall was responsible for convening meetings and setting out the agenda. This created the impression that the Roundtable was a municipal project and that the mayor had final say. Lastly, only three COCODEs, all of which represented urban neighborhoods, were invited to participate in the Environmental Roundtable—and even then, their participation was marginal in comparison with the local organizations, municipal leaders, and outside technicians.

The intense politicization of the protected-area process in the San Cristóbal case illustrates one problem with environmental capital-based development initiatives in weak institutional environments. High-profile environmental initiatives, including the establishment of protected areas, attract the attention of international funders and become very visible types of political victories that play well in the media. For these reasons, one can extract substantial political rents from such projects. In stronger institutional environments where civil society is better equipped to hold government accountable and institutionalized checks help prevent collusion, tension between community members and local government is often productive and creative rather than detrimental to the development process (see Peterman 2000 for a discussion of creative tension in the context of community organizing in Chicago). For this reason the community capitals framework may not always translate perfectly across institutional environments or national borders, and political institutional endowments may outweigh economic factor endowments in cases where they are in conflict. This may be in part because the multifunctionality of natural resources causes different populations to conceive of these resources in distinct ways.

In addition to the Marxian categories of use and exchange value, certain environmental assets, in certain contexts, may also possess symbolic value, as the case of Laguna Chichoj demonstrates. Symbolic value is determined by the significance of an object or phenomenon within the collective consciousness of a given social group. This significance is separate from the material utility that is derived from use-valuable commodities and the monetary utility of exchange-valuable commodities. Symbolic value can be operationalized when an individual or group invokes representatively valuable objects or phenomena, resulting in the attribution of credit. That credit can then serve the credited in materially important ways, such as forgiveness or support. A natural resource has use value as an organ of an ecosystem, use value as a provider of environmental services to the human population, exchange value as a commodified amenity, and symbolic value that can be leveraged for material gain. Each of these ways of conceptualizing an organ of the landscape is a different lens that cuts along the contours of different social groups. Peasant groups that are less integrated into the global economy than other social groups may depend on environmental services that the landscape provides as a dimension of their livelihood strategies. The COCODES in San Cristobal Verapaz viewed the Laguna through the service lens. To these groups, the lake possessed use value. In contrast, the local and national elites who constituted the Environmental Roundtable for the Rescue of Laguna Chichoj viewed the lake through the symbolic lens. In their eyes, the lake was a political tool that could be symbolically manipulated to extract political rents. The third lens, the capital lens, conceptualized the lake as a commodity to be traded, and thus endowed the object with exchange value. Both the service and symbolic lenses are characteristic of, although by no means endemic to, some developing countries where partially subsistence-level livelihoods and political rent-seeking are widespread phenomena. The capital lens, on the other hand, is more common in the global north, perhaps because the historically larger leisure class understands the landscape in part as a recreational apparatus.

Multifunctionality means that natural resources, in particular amenities with high visibility, signify different things to different groups in a community. David Marcouiller and Greg Clendenning (2005) characterize amenities by high-income elasticity of demand, but that is the case only when a resource is conceptualized through the capital lens as deriving its value through exchange. When the same resource is conceptualized by rural peasants through the service lens, demand is considerably less income-elastic. In this case, and others like it where political rent-seeking in natural resource management intervenes in genuine community-led efforts to develop around environmental capital, the power structure is not acting in the interests of the population. This is more likely to happen in weak political institutional environments where civil society possesses less leverage over its elected officials.

Jeffrey Klein and Steven Wolf (2007) apply the concept of multifunctionality beyond agriculture to landscapes in general. They find that in the Northern Forest of New York State there are distinct orientations regarding forest management. Further, they find that "political economic factors shape the relative value individuals place on . . . forests" (Klein and Wolf 2007:414). This work parallels, to some extent, the typology of lenses advanced here. However, this typology is far from exhaustive and additional literature must develop it further.

This case and its lessons affirm earlier research that natural resource issues, by virtue of their contentious multifunctionality and unique visibility, lend themselves to political entrepreneurialism that can undermine genuine community initiatives (Walker and Hurley 2004). Environmental capital-based development has the potential to serve as an important component of comprehensive community development planning, but the institutional conditions must be right to maximize the potential of this strategy. Where the right mix of factor endowments, strong political institutions and strong civil society are in place, leveraging environmental capital can constitute an effective form of asset building, which can shore up community economic autonomy, contribute to quality of life, and enhance ecosystems. Nevertheless, the San Cristóbal case suggests that although many rural areas in the developing world possess favorable economic conditions for effective environmental capital-based development, the relative strength of political institutions and civil society must be also considered as a determining factor in the outcomes of such initiatives.

List of Acronyms

ASOVERAPAZ: Asociación Verapaz (Verapaz Association), the local nonprofit organization that spearheaded the process of declaring the Laguna protected

CATIE: Centro Agronómico Tropical para la Investigación y Enseñaza (Tropical Agronomical Center for Research and Teaching), the Costa Rican organization that disbursed and oversaw the financing of the program of protected-area declaration that sponsored the Laguna Chichoj initiative

COCODE: Consejo Comunitario de Desarrollo (Community Development Council), a legally mandated grassroots development organization that operates on the submunicipal level of the urban neighborhood or rural hamlet

CONAP: Consejo Nacional de Áreas Protegidas (National Council of Protected Areas), the state agency that manages Guatemala's system of protected areas

DGIS: Netherlands Directorate General of Development Cooperation, the government development agency of the Netherlands responsible for underwriting the program of protected-area declaration that sponsored the Laguna Chichoj initiative

FONAPAZ: Fondo Nacional para la Paz (National Peace Fund)

GANA: Gran Alianza Nacional (Great National Alliance), the political party that held the presidency for the 2003–2007 term

GASAL: Grupo Asociado Salvemos al Lago (Associated Group "Let's Save the Lake"), a local nonprofit organization primarily concerned with removing invasive plant species

from the Laguna and also part of the Roundtable initiative
to declare the Laguna protected

GSM: Grupo Sierra Madre, the environmental consulting firm
hired to conduct the technical plan for the protected-area
declaration of the Laguna Chichoj watershed

INAB: Instituto Nacional de Bosques (National Forest
Institute)

MARN: Ministerio de Ambiente y Recursos Naturales (Ministry of Environment and Natural Resources)

OECD: Organization for Economic Co-operation and
Development

SCEP: Secretaria de Coordinación Ejecutiva de la Presidencia
(Secretariat of Executive Coordination of the Presidency)

Notes

1. In this chapter we refer to environmental and natural capital interchangeably. We use the term *environmental capital* throughout, but where we refer to another text that uses the term *natural capital*, use also use the term *natural capital*.

2. Laguna Chichoj is the proper name of the small lake that is the focal point of the proposed protected area discussed here. The Spanish word *laguna* refers to a small, freshwater body of water, whereas the false English cognate *lagoon* refers to a saline bay or ocean inlet. Here we call this pond *Laguna*, referring to its proper name.

References

Bond, Matthew R. 2003. *"The Power of Municipal Development Plans: An Examination of Their Relevance and Impact in Guatemala."* Masters Thesis, Department of Urban and Regional Planning, Virginia Polytechnic Institute and State University, Blacksburg, VA. Retrieved August 28, 2007. http://scholar.lib.vt.edu/theses/available/etd-01202004-092511/unrestricted/MBondThesis-FinalDraft.pdf.

Bourdieu, Pierre. 1986. "The forms of capital." Pp. 241–258 in *Handbook of Theory and Research for the Sociology of Education*, edited by J.G. Richardson. Westport, CT: Greenwood Press.

Brocklesby, Mary Ann, and Eleanor Fisher. 2003. "Community development in sustainable livelihoods approaches: An introduction." *Journal of the Community Development Society* 38:185–198.

Coleman, James S. 1988. "Social capital in the creation of human capital." *American Journal of Sociology* 94:S95–S120.

Crowe, Jessica. 2006. "Community economic development strategies in rural Washington: Toward a synthesis of natural and social capital." *Rural Sociology* 71:573–596.

Flora, Cornelia B., and Jan L. Flora. 2008. *Rural Communities: Legacy and Change.* Boulder, CO: Westview Press.

Flora, Jan L. 1998. "Social capital and communities of place." *Rural Sociology* 63:481–506.

Granovetter, Mark. 1974. *Getting a Job: A Study of Contacts and Careers.* Cambridge, MA: Harvard University Press.

Green, Gary P., Leann M. Tigges, and Irene Browne. 1995. "Social resources, job search, and poverty in Atlanta." *Research in Community Sociology* 5:161–182.

Green, Gary Paul, and Anna Haines. 2007. *Asset Building and Community Development,* 2nd Edition. Thousand Oaks, CA: Sage Publications.

Grupo Sierra Madre. 2006. *Informe al Estudio Técnico Final.* Guatemala City: Consejo Nacional de Áreas Protegidas.

Instituto Nacional de Estadística. 2004. *Datos de Alta Verapaz, Características Generales de la Población y Habitación.* Guatemala City.

Klein, Jeffrey A. and Steven A. Wolf. 2007. "Toward multifunctional landscapes: Cross-sectional analysis of management priorities in New York's northern forest." *Rural Sociology* 72:391–417.

Kretzmann, John, and John McKnight. 1993. *Building Communities from the Inside Out: A Path Toward Finding and Mobilizing a Community's Assets.* Evanston, IL: Center for Urban Affairs and Policy Research, Northwestern University.

Marcouiller, David W., and Greg Clendenning. 2005. "The supply of natural amenities: Moving from empirical anecdotes to a theoretical basis." Pp. 6–32 in *Amenities and Rural Development: Theory, Methods and Public Policy,* edited by Gary Paul Green, Steven Deller, and David Marcouiller. Cheltenham, U.K.: Edward Elgar Publishing.

Marx, Karl (1976 [orig. 1867]) *Capital,* vol. 1. New York: Vintage Books.

McChesny, Fred S. 1987. "Rent extraction and rent creation in the economic theory of regulation." *Journal of Legal Studies* 16:101–118.

Méndez, Pablo Escobar. 2007. Mayor, Aguacatan, Gautemala; personal communication with Michael Dougherty (June).

Palmer, Elizabeth. 2007. Returned Peace Corps Volunteer; Tecpan, Guatemala; personal communication with Michael L. Dougherty (August).

Peterman, William. 2000. *Neighborhood Planning and Community-Based Development: The Potential and Limits of Grassroots Action.* Thousand Oaks, CA: Sage Publications.

Potschin, M.B., and R.H. Haines-Young. 2003. "Improving the quality of environmental assessments using the concept of natural capital: A case study from southern Germany." *Landscape and Urban Planning* 63:93–108.

Putnam, Robert. 1993. *Making Democracy Work: Civic Traditions in Modern Italy.* Princeton, NJ: Princeton University Press.

República de Guatemala. 1989. *Ley de Áreas Protegidas.* Retrieved on August 28, 2007. www.mem.gob.gt/Portal/Documents/Documents/2005-09/418/77/ley%20areas%20protegidas.pdf.

Rubio, Fernando E, Lorena Moreira de Pastor, Gunther Carranza, Maria del Carmen Aceña, and Jorge Lavarreda. 2003. "Monitoreo de Obras de Infraestructura de los Consejos de Desarrollo Urbano y Rural." Retrieved on August 28, 2007. www.congreso.gob.gt/plumainvitada/10.pdf.

Secretaría General de la Planificación. 2002. *Mapas de Pobreza en Guatemala al 2002.* Retrieved on August 28, 2007. http://ine.gob.gt/pdf/MAPAS_POBREZA2002.pdf.

Shuman, Michael H. 1998. *Going Local: Creating Self-Reliant Communities in a Global Age.* New York: The Free Press.

Walker, Peter A., and Patrick T. Hurley. 2004. "Collaboration derailed: The politics of 'community-based' resource management in Nevada County." *Society and Natural Resources* 17:735–751.

5 Linking Cultural Capital Conceptions to Asset-Based Community Development

RHONDA PHILLIPS AND
GORDON SHOCKLEY

Introduction

Cultural capital is an increasingly popular topic both from perspectives of economic-oriented analysis and in the context of community-based applications exploring societal accumulation and its outcomes. With its ascendancy, conceptual ideas about cultural capital and perceptions of it are changing. Prior definitions focused on arts and heritage, but new understandings and applications are now continually evolving.

Beyond arts and heritage, cultural capital encompasses various elements to include "diverse traditions, values, place, and social history. . . . The stock of cultural capital, both tangible and intangible, is what we inherit from past generations and what we will pass onto future generations. Overall, it leads to quality of life and better knowledge of ourselves" (Creative City Network of Canada 2008:2). Cultural capital can thus be seen to hold much potential to influence the broad sphere of community development.

Cultural capital is distinct from, yet related to, economic capital, which briefly is defined as cash and other economic assets. It is important to recognize cultural capital's instrumental and intrinsic value and its role in development. The World Commission on Culture and Development has made this clear in their seminal report, *Our Creative Diversity*, which strives to protect cultural assets and diversity from development patterns that limit or endanger cultural capital (World Commission on Culture and Diversity 1996:14). The need for development worldwide is clear and pressing, yet the need to avoid reducing "culture to a subsidiary position as a mere promoter of economic growth" is paramount. Further, UNESCO adopted the "Universal Declaration on Cultural Diversity" to bring attention to the vital dimensions of culture. In Article 3, they define cultural diversity as a factor of development:

> Cultural diversity widens the range of options open to everyone; it is one of the roots of development, understood not simply in terms of economic growth, but also as a means to achieve a more satisfactory intellectual, emotional, moral and spiritual existence (UNESCO 2001: Article 3).

Cultural capital is also related to social capital, which consists of relationship-based resources, or as Bridger and Alter (2006:6) define it, "trust and norms of reciprocity emerging from repeated and regularized interactions that are bounded in space and time." It is this relationship with social capital that ties in directly with notions of sustainability. As noted by the Creative City Network of Canada (2008), culture is gradually emerging out of the realm of social sustainability and is being recognized as having a separate, distinct, and integral role in sustainable development. Cultural sustainability implies that change occurs when cultural values are respected. Further, the Creative City Network of Canada (2008) maintains that discussions of sustainability must include an understanding of culture as well as of the place in which it occurs, so that community and geographic context are not ignored. Serious discussions of sustainability mandate in-depth exploration of the nuances of each situation, and preservation of both the environment and culture must be balanced with practices.

Because cultural capital may be overlooked in the process of sustainable development, a shift in the approaches in which all types of capital are managed and used is needed (Cochrane 2006). Cultural sustainability thus becomes integrated with other dimensions of sustainability and community development.

As cultural capital's importance is increasingly recognized, viewpoints are evolving to take into consideration the full spectrum of cultural-capital dimensions and to avoid a reductionist perspective. This is evident from the "economic" viewpoint, as well as seen in Ginsburgh and Throsby's 2006 *Handbook of the Economics of Art and Culture*, where the relationships between economic value and cultural value are explored from a variety of perspectives, including economics and management, art history, art philosophy, public policy, sociology, and law. The volume illustrates how cultural capital bridges many disciplines and plays a vital development role. This integral relationship of economics and cultural capital can be described as including both the *stock* of assets and a *flow* of capital services over time (Ginsburg and Throsby 2006). This essentially translates into two types of perceived value: either economic or cultural.

Cultural capital can be viewed from different perspectives and has important roles to play in development. In this chapter, the conceptions of cultural capital will focus on the sociological and economic perspectives, examining the work of a major theorist in the area, David Throsby. It will then explore links from theory to practice, discussing how conceptualizations are applied in asset-based community development (ABCD) approaches. It is not the intent of this work to discuss inequities regarding cultural capital, but rather to explore how conceptualizations relate to application.

Conceptualizing Cultural Capital

Pierre Bourdieu, along with Jean-Claude Passeron, is credited with first articulating cultural capital as a sociological concept. Most notably, Bourdieu expressed cultural capital in the context of personal interest in and experience with prestigious cultural resources. Familiarity with traditional high culture forms a defining characteristic of individuals occupying high-status positions within a society (Jeanotte 2003). It is very much a microlevel conception, focusing on individual interaction. Throsby, in contrast to Bourdieu, views cultural capital as a macro-idea that factors into social life at the level of societal accumulation of cultural phenomena beyond that of individual social interaction.

"Cultural capital in an economic sense," Throsby (2001:44) writes, "can provide a means of representing culture that enables both tangible and intangible manifestations of culture to be articulated as long-lasting stores of value and providers of benefits for individuals and groups." Serving as a repository of value as a stock and facilitating the flow of cultural services are the two primary functions of Throsbian cultural capital. *Stock* "refers to the quantity of such capital in existence at a given time. . . . This capital stock gives rise over time to a *flow* of services that may be consumed or may be used to produce further goods and services" (Throsby 2001:46). Stocks and flows are exogenous to the individual, however. Tangible cultural capital includes buildings, structures, sites and locations endowed with cultural significance and artworks and artifacts existing as private goods, such as paintings, sculptures, and other objects. Intangible cultural capital is the set of ideas, practices, beliefs, traditions, and values that serve to identify and bind together a given group of people. Much like the intangible and tangible aspects of nature (an analogy Throsby himself repeatedly makes), Throsbian cultural capital is a stock of objects and embodied ideas as well as the services that flow from them. Throsbian cultural capital thus serves as a massive cultural resource that individuals and groups can draw upon in Bourdieuan acquisitions, conversions, and reproduction strategies, but it is an exogenous stock whose flow originates upstream, far above and beyond individual, or micro-level, social interaction.

Throsbian cultural capital is consistent with many common notions of the existence of cultural objects and artifacts to a particular society. At the founding of the National Endowment for the Arts in 1965 in the United States, for example, Henry Hyde referred to cultural property as a commons. It is "the "creative wealth of the past" that now "exists in the present and on which we continue to build artistically and intellectually" (quoted in Campbell 1999:5). Similarly, the Center for Arts and Culture, a once-independent arts policy think tank currently supported by Americans for the Arts, conceived of America's culture as "a national resource, the accumulated capital of America's ingenuity and creativity" (Center for Arts and Culture 2001:180). A.R. Morato (2003:250–251) identifies culture as "a significant resource within the general economic and political sphere." The notion that a society accumulates larger cultural phenomena over time is not new.

Other commentators relate stocks of larger, accumulated cultural phenomena to the concept of nationhood. "Art, architecture, literature, theatre, dance and music," Radbourne and Fraser (1996:9) write, "provide some of the most translatable and permanent media for the expression of national identity." Cultural capital in this sense can contribute to such areas as international prestige, the preservation and reinforcement of cultural identity, education of the young, and the preservation of cultural evidence to foster culture (Shubik 1999). Therefore, insofar as Throsby is referring to a preexisting stock of objects—be they artwork or national heritage, for instance—he is operationalizing his conception of cultural capital at the macrolevel of societal accumulation.

Throsby (1995:2001) has conceptualized a set of cultural policies for the sustainable development of cultural capital at the societal level. The weakness of Throsby's macrolevel conception of cultural capital is that, like most macroeconomic concepts, it neglects individual interaction. Throsby's conception recognizes that a group of artifacts and embodiments exist in any modern culture, such as historical buildings, works of art, public rituals, and shared beliefs. In this way, Throsby's conception of cultural capital conforms to our intuitions and experience of modern culture. The problem, however, lies in Throsby's neglect of the origin and formation of cultural capital. Throsbian cultural capital exists exogenously—that is, as given, already created, always maintained, and perhaps even automatically augmented. But it leaves many crucial issues unaddressed. Where does cultural capital come from? How is it maintained? How is it acquired and used in social interactions?

Most answers to these questions can be answered only at the level of the individual and social interaction. Individuals interact in social space. Individuals create and experience art. In Bourdieu's terms, individuals acquire, convert, and strategize to reproduce cultural capital. The exogenous treatment of any phenomena is mute to these vital considerations at the level of the individual. In prior work, Throsby (1994) sees works of art as cultural goods endogenously consumed at the level of the individual. As discussed above, he seems to have completely refocused on a macrolevel conception of cultural capital that has important implications for community development. Throsby's conception of cultural capital at the macrolevel of societal accumulation profoundly differs from Bourdieu's microconception of cultural capital at the level of individual interaction. How might the idea of cultural capital, one that reflects this societal level, be operationalized?

From Theory to Practice: Exploring Cultural Capital in Asset-Based Community Development

How can communities benefit from conceptions of cultural capital? What is to be learned from these varying viewpoints, and can they be integrated into ABCD? Green and Haines (2007:vii) define ABCD as

> ... a planned effort to produce assets that increase the capacity of residents to improve their quality of life.... Building on a community's assets rather than focusing on its needs for future development is the basic approach of asset-based community development; by focusing on successes and small triumphs instead of looking to what is missing or negative about a place, a positive community outlook and vision for the future can be fostered.

Understanding the critical aspect of assets within this framework is crucial to ABCD. Assets are considered capital in communities in whatever form present. In their influential work on community development, Kretzmann and McKnight (1993) present assets as the gifts, skills, and capacities of individuals, associations, and institutions.

These assets can be categorized into the expected economic, environmental, and social capital forms, as well as physical, cultural, and political forms (Green and Haines 2007). Emery and Flora (2006:20–21) offer a slightly different version of assets. Their version defines assets in the following manner:

- Cultural capital reflects the way people know the world and how they act within it, as well as their traditions and language. It influences what voices are heard and listened to, which voices have influence in what areas, and how innovation and creativity emerge and are fostered.
- Natural capital refers to assets that abide in a particular location, including resources, amenities, and natural beauty.

- Human capital consists of the skills and abilities of people to develop and enhance their resources and to access outside resources and bodies of knowledge in order to support community building, including leadership development.
- Social capital comprises the connections among people and organizations or the social interaction needed to make things happen.
- Political capital reflects access to power, organizations, and connections to resources both internal and external to the community.
- Built capital includes the physical infrastructure of a community.
- Financial capital consists of the financial resources available to invest in community capacity building—that is, building businesses in the private and social sectors by supporting entrepreneurship and increasing wealth in communities.

Cultural capital is critical to the ABCD process because of its nature and influence as forces of creativity and innovation. Indeed, the attention paid to generating creative economies is widespread and reflects a tradition of methodological individualism in which interaction among individuals is seen to result in emergent phenomena at the system level. In other words, the individual's actions influence a larger arena, or system, at some point. The system level can be taken to mean communities; thus, interaction among individuals in the cultural-capital realm can result in larger results (phenomena) for communities. Evidence of this conceptualization of cultural capital is not hard to find. For example, arts-based development outcomes are in evidence globally. They occur when individual artists are attracted to locations where conditions exist to foster creativity; a synergistic effect is achieved as more artists are attracted to locate there and a localization economy is created. Eventually, local government or social-support organizations respond, thereby increasing the effect and impact.

Cultural-Capital Vignettes

Numerous examples exist where this development trajectory of creating a localization economy has occurred, including small rural communities that have emerged as artist colonies or communities such as Bisbee, Arizona or Colquitt, Georgia. Bisbee is a high-altitude desert town on the Arizona-Mexico border, prosperous in the Old West days of the late 1800s and early 1900s, with a population reaching nearly ten thousand. Noted for its famous Copper Queen Mine and hotels, it was a major mining town. With the decline of mining, its population plummeted by the 1970s. It was not until several artists located there in the 1990s to take advantage of low-priced housing and studio facilities that more activities began to be attracted to the town. Its Victorian architecture, art deco Courthouse, and hilly terrain drew artists who renovated properties and helped develop its thriving, historic, downtown cultural core. Now, it is a flourishing community of just over six thousand, attracting many visitors to experience its unique arts venues and ambience. There are numerous art galleries, and art is integrated into retail stores, such as a historic bicycle shop. The town's unusual environment also includes such attractions as a historic popular-culture art hotel in the form of vintage Airstream travel trailers. Firmly recognized as an artist's colony, it has built its foundation on culturally based development.

Colquitt, Georgia (population two thousand) is another example of how individuals coming together to share cultural capital can rebuild a community. This shared capital is in the form of storytelling, bringing together residents of all ages to preserve their heritage. Colquitt was a victim of the decline of rural agriculture and was suffering from a depressed economy and tense racial relations. One thing the residents had in common was their Southern heritage and love of storytelling. In the early 1990s, a team of volunteers began collecting oral histories from the residents, and this grew into a play, *Swamp Gravy,* that has generated a phenomenon of attracting tens of thousands of visitors per year to partake in semiannual Swamp Gravy festivals. Outcomes have included reduced racial tensions, with all races and ages participating in the play, and a sense of pride in the community. The Museum of Southern Culture was developed as an outgrowth of the Swamp Gravy festival, as well as the Swamp Gravy Institute, an arts service organization. Other programs have emerged too, including the New Life Learning Center to serve school-age children with arts-based programs. Colquitt is an excellent example of the transformative power of arts and culture when applied in the community context.

Sometimes in artist colonies, the phenomenon generated develops beyond its original intent as demand increases for properties located in the highly desirable arts areas. This can be seen in urban areas, particularly in high-demand centers where artists are displaced as wealthier residents seek to locate in the arts areas. Portland, Oregon's Pearl District downtown is one such example where old warehouses were initially used as affordable studio space by artists and, as demand increased, more upscale reuse began to supplant former uses. The district is now home to major national specialty retail chains as well as expensive residential and commercial uses. The Pearl District is now viewed as Portland's premier urban-chic neighborhood, with upscale townhouses, lofts, and condos. Infill construction is often presold in the district. Although there are still some artists in the district, the increase in the cost of property has displaced others. The issue of displacement and related outcomes is not dealt with in Throsby's macroconception, but it is certainly an issue within community development.

Throsby's conception of cultural capital is a macroconception that factors into social life at the level of societal accumulation of cultural phenomena beyond that of individual social interaction. This societal accumulation can be fostered with deliberate policy and investments by the social sectors (government and nonprofit), usually in conjunction with the private sectors (artists, businesses, and private foundations, for example). In some areas, it is termed *community cultural development*. In others, it is referred to as *arts-based development*. Either way, it seeks to encourage creative partnerships and collaborations for positive development and change. Although Throsby's work considers cultural capital to exist exogenously as given—already created, maintained, and perhaps even automatically augmented—it leaves crucial issues unaddressed, as discussed above. This is where deliberate action in the social sectors can guide the process in achieving societal accumulation. Witness the numerous communities that are intentionally developing cultural-capital development plans and policies.

The City of Clearwater was one of the first communities in the rapidly growing state of Florida to develop an extensive cultural-development plan linked to economic and community development goals. In 2002, Clearwater conducted a cultural-planning process, resulting in the *Clearwater Cultural Plan*, which serves as a guiding document for integrating cultural assets into community processes and activities. Clearwater also included a cultural-development element in the overall comprehensive plan for the City, ensuring culture's significance in the planning and development process at the local government level. These and similar actions are intentional societal accumulation of cultural capital. They recognize the value of integrating culture as an asset into overall development and planning.

To help coordinate the integration of culture with community, Clearwater established a Cultural Affairs Division charged with the mission of enhancing cultural life for residents and visitors. Activities include sculpture and other public art commissions and placement throughout the community. Additionally, the Division coordinates with other organizations to provide art for the elderly and for youth as well as keeping culture and the arts at the forefront of community interest and civic leadership.

Clearwater developed this extensive cultural-development plan and commitment to policy, activities, and public investments because they believed that cultural-based development will enhance quality-of-life experiences for both residents and visitors. Results have included development of the perception of Clearwater as an "arts-oriented" community as well as increasing visitors for arts and cultural venues and activities. Residents have indicated enjoyment and satisfaction with the emphasis on arts and culture, not only in terms of increased venues and activities but also the overall increased cultural ambience of the community. While these aspects of community may not be readily quantifiable, they reflect qualitative dimensions of community.

Linking Cultural Capital and Asset-Based Community Development

A case in point of a community that explicitly links Throsby's macro-level conception of cultural capital to ABCD outcomes is Bellow Falls, Vermont. This example might also be reflective of Throsby's idea that deliberate societal accumulation of cultural capital can be prompted by policies and culture-sector investments. Bellows Falls, Vermont (population 3,700) is a classic case of how arts-based economic development programming, policies, and strategies can result in societal accumulation of cultural capital.

An incorporated village since 1834 and located within another town, Rockingham, the community has a rich history replete with a canal, textile mills, and many historic properties. It is the home of the first chartered canal in the United States, built between 1791 and 1802 and still running through the village today. It has long been a popular site for a community, as evidenced by prehistoric petroglyphs carved into the rocks near the river, and in later times by its abundant Victorian homes and distinctive town square lined with red brick buildings. Bellows Falls grew and prospered in economic terms because of railroad activities and, later, paper mills. Because of serious economic decline since the Great Depression, Bellows Falls by 1997 had become a shadow of its former self. With crumbling brick factories, Victorian homes in decay, the downtown railroad hotel closed, the majority of storefronts empty, and only one track in the large rail yard used, it was developmentally defunct.

Despite these challenges, within a few short years the village was presented as a model of community development for using creative ideas, the arts, and cooperative local citizen efforts to revitalize itself. The Vermont Community Development Association held a day-long conference in 2000 to showcase the village as a prime example of these endeavors as well as of a community using a wide variety of funding sources for redevelopment (Smith 2000:B1).

How did they accomplish these feats within such a short time? At its lowest point, several groups of citizens decided that something had to be done. A grassroots community group called Our Town formed to restore the historic clock tower, raising funds and providing a symbol of hope to the village's revitalization. The second group to form was the Front Porch Theatre Company. But it was the formation of the Rockingham Arts and Museum Project (RAMP), founded by an artist who relocated from New York City to Bellows Falls, that spurred a comprehensive arts-based development effort. RAMP's mission is to (1) develop awareness of the arts, (2) create vitality in the community with the arts, and (3) demonstrate that the arts favorably impact the local economy, with the program's success relying on developing effective partnerships. RAMP developed partnerships with the other two community groups as well as groups external to Bellows Falls. They decided from the beginning to integrate art into overall community development, building on assets inherent in the community. The overall community development theme is "Art Makes a Difference!" The village adopted this as their motto, and citizens were galvanized into action as they restored properties, attracting more artists and galleries and pushing local government to incorporate art into overall comprehensive planning and development (Phillips 2002b:20).

Numerous arts venues and programs have been developed. Yet the key to their success has been that they have taken it beyond offering arts events to a true comprehensive community development effort. A major focus has been infrastructure improvements, including renovation of the historic Exner Block. Built in the 1870s, it now provides space for artist studios and living space, as well as retail space. The project required funding from a variety of sources—partnerships were used to develop the creative funding mix of public and private sources. Murals have been painted in the town, funded by state and National Endowment for the Arts grants. Other projects have included construction of a multimodal transportation center, linking the historic rail station and the Green Mountain Flyer (a historic train) to scenic trails, including a grist mill, the petroglyphs, and Victorian architecture. Historic street lighting has been installed; efforts to purchase and stabilize a historic hotel are underway, and a Waypoint Interpretative Center has been funded as part of the Connecticut River Scenic Byway project.

Throsbian cultural capital, and cultural-capital theory in general, makes sense of Bellow Falls' deliberate and persistent integration of the arts into the village's planning and development. Creating opportunities for residents and tourists alike to engage and participate in the arts facilitated the microlevel development of Bourdieuan cultural capital, which over time would accumulate into macrolevel Throsbian intangible cultural capital. At the same time, Bellow Falls' ABCD approach promoted the growth of Throsbian tangible cultural capital. The arts-based strategies have influenced all manners of community development, including the notable renovation of the historic Exner Block. Providing affordable artist studio and living space as well as storefronts has resulted in an influx of artists and other new residents. Additionally, new retail establishments, including restaurants and coffee houses, as well as a number of galleries, generate a flow of services income from the stock of cultural capital. The town serves as an arts incubator that encourages arts-based development throughout. The results are an accumulation of benefits at the community or societal level, based on cultural capital (that is, arts-based development programs, policies, and outcomes).

Sustainability Considerations

Community-level cultural-capital development can also be considered within the sustainable-development framework, especially when it builds on inherent assets in communities to accomplish the desires of citizens. The Creative City Network of Canada describes these approaches as consistent with sustainability principles by supporting a community culture, empowering residents, and strengthening cultural infrastructure and participation in a community. Community cultural development has also been linked to other sustainable community development initiatives, such as health, affordable housing, education, youth, poverty, education, policy, and planning (Creative City Network of Canada 2008). Using a cultural lens in all these areas is an emerging component of sustainable development. Community cultural development is a community-building tool that promotes a sense of place, empowerment, and public participation—all key components in the sustainable community development field. Community cultural development and sustainable community development share common values, principals, key elements, and dynamics, and can help inform emerging cultural-sustainability models.

What are some of the benefits of such an approach for communities to consider? There are several, reflecting the underlying premises of ABCD in the community cultural-development context. The following provides a summary of the key aspects of the approach (Creative City Network of Canada 2008:3):

1. *It focuses on arts-based solutions, rather than on identifying problems.* This is consistent with the basic premise of ABCD as a positive orientation toward community devel-

opment where the assets are identified as the major focus, rather than issues or problems.

2. *It involves policymakers in the planning and development process.* Policymakers are instrumental in the process to ensure that action can be taken at the appropriate level. In addition, the assumption is that not only policymakers will be a vital part of the process, but that residents and other stakeholders in the community are participants as well.

3. *It forms and maintains new social networks with organizations, groups, artists, and government.* These networks are important to build both bridging and bonding social-capital connections, enabling effective communication.

4. *It creates and maintains public spaces that draw people together.* The provision of space is critical to the development and use of cultural assets.

5. *It supports multiculturalism.* Encouraging participation and provision of culturally based assets (venues, programs, and so forth) to all is crucial and enhances both contributions to and enjoyment of assets.

6. *It integrates local customs, crafts, and practices into education.* It is important to include the local assets as the foundation for culturally based development, as this not only serves the inclusionary goal of ABCD but also provides a basis on which to build culturally based development approaches and venues.

7. *It uses arts and culture as a tool for regeneration and sustainability.* The value of cultural capital as a basis for development and community regeneration is becoming increasingly recognized.

8. *It enhances residents' ability to work and communicate with others.* Art can serve as a highly effective form of communication and is a true boundary spanner in terms of being able to reach across diverse groups.

9. *It builds community identity and pride.* The integration of art and culture is an important aspect of identity and can serve as the basis for answering the question, "Who are we as a community?"

10. *It supports positive community norms, such as cultural understanding and free expression.* Again, arts and culture foster communication, and in turn the ability to communicate leads to greater understanding.

11. *It improves human capital, skills, and creative abilities in communities.* Creative skills and abilities have direct links to opportunities in other spheres, including economic and social spheres.

12. *It increases opportunities for individuals to become more involved in the arts.* Participation in the arts engenders myriad benefits, not the least of which is an enhancement in the quality of life.

13. *It contributes to the resiliency and sustainability of a community or people.* This has been shown over and over again, with arts and culture serving as the glue that binds a people or community together in both challenging and prosperous times.

14. *It reduces delinquency in high-risk youth.* The inclusion of youth in arts-and-culture-based programs and activities has been shown to reduce negative behaviors and to encourage positive participation.

15. *It integrates the community into community art projects.* Arts-and-culture-based development approaches truly need the support and participation of the overall community, with inclusion of a diverse array of residents and other stakeholders. Because of its nature, it enables a community-wide approach with benefits for all.

Again, there are numerous examples of targeting outcomes like these in programs aimed at protecting and enhancing cultural capital. These examples include developing community-based arts business incubators or cooperatives, for example, where individual artists are brought together in a supporting, nurturing environment and provided with marketing assistance (Phillips 2002a). For example, the Department of Culture and Arts, Western Australia (ArtsWA) worked with the Artists' Foundation of Western Australia in a collaborative partnership to develop the skills of indigenous artists and provide commissioning opportunities for their work and employment opportunities in the cultural sector (Department of Culture and the Arts 2003). Services include bringing together the resources of an Aboriginal Arts Advisory Panel along with local, state, and federal government agencies in partnership with private-sector companies.

Economic Considerations

Bringing these ideas back to economic considerations, we should examine the areas where policy and culture intersect. Throsby (2006:18) discusses these intersections and lists the areas most impacted:

- Cultural industries as sources of innovation, growth and structural changes in economies
- Appropriate levels of government support of arts and culture, including direct (grants) and indirect (tax-related) means of support
- Trade policy for cultural goods and services
- Public or private partnerships to preserve cultural heritage
- The role of arts and culture in job and income generation in communities, including those affected by declining economies
- Legal and economic questions concerning the regulation of intellectual property in cultural goods and services

These points illustrate the intersection of community development (the policy perspective) and culture. For example, much attention is paid to the contribution of culture industries in our economies (witness the rise of creative economies). This has spurred the examination of public expenditures on arts and culture, including the shift in thinking from arts as activities to be subsidized to arts as an investment by local, regional, and national governments. The attention has benefited culture in other ways too. For example, more interest is now paid to culture as assets, including the preservation of heritage and other cultural links as valuable community assets. At both the local and regional levels, the impact on jobs and income has received more attention, too, as research (and recognition) emerges on the value of arts-based development to economies.

The appeal and potential of culture's influence on community development is being pursued in myriad contexts, from the smallest hamlet to the largest urban concentrations. Witness tiny (population 450) Jerome, Arizona's positioning itself as an artist colony in its isolated mountain location, drawing in thousands of visitors a year to partake in its unique culture. Entire countries are positioning themselves within the culture-as-community development framework. Scotland is presenting the Creative Scotland Bill to Parliament, hoping to establish a national-level cultural-development body. This entity would oversee and promote culture's role in development and continue to enhance the importance of Scotland's creative industries, whose impact on the economy is £5 billion annually.

There are several ways to operationalize the idea of Throsby's cultural capital. Although much remains to be investigated, it is clear that conceptions such as those presented here can provide insight into ABCD.

Summary

The conceptualization of cultural capital as societal accumulation becomes a vital component as both an input in the process of ABCD and an outcome. Throsby's work in this area has prompted an exploration of the varying perspectives of cultural capital. His definition of cultural capital is as both a stock of assets and a flow of capital that gives rise to economic and cultural values. Throsbian cultural capital can represent cultural resources that are drawn upon for societal accumulation. It is this societal accumulation that holds particular relevance for ABCD. These conceptions are approached with an overriding question: How can theory translate into practice so that community development outcomes can be realized?

The tying of cultural-capital conceptions to ABCD can be used to explore how society and communities can move from conceptualization to application. A notable feature is that cultural capital is considered critical to the ABCD process through its nature and influence as a force of creativity and innovation. This in turn is the major foundation on which arts-based development approaches are built and implemented. This effect can be seen in arts communities in particular. Interaction among individuals (artists) can result in larger impacts at the community level, or societal accumulation. It can also include explicit policy actions by the social sector to further encourage desirable community development outcomes. It is this bringing together of cultural capital with other forms of capital—social, political, built, financial, human, and natural—to achieve development goals that represents potential for ABCD applications.

Culture capital can indeed serve as the basis for community development, and many cases exist where positive benefits have been generated. There are also obstacles to promoting cultural capital's use as an asset-based development tool. One occurs when cultural assets are not treated as a community resource and are instead overly "commodified" to the point that residents may not realize benefits. For example, this may happen in cases where tourism is used as the basis for development and where culture is commercialized or commodified with little regard for the authenticity of the local culture. Other obstacles include the lack of diverse participation in a community, leaving some residents or groups out of the process. This can lead to construction of culture-based development approaches that do not reflect the desires of the greater community, as well as to a lack of support for implementation. It is important for communities to be aware of obstacles should they pursue culture-based development.

As discussed, there are varying approaches to cultural-capital conceptions, and the interface of economic analysis with community development applications can yield insight into how benefits can be gained by communities. ABCD, with its holistic framework of considering a range of assets beyond economic, is readily compatible with macrolevel and microlevel conceptions of cultural capital. Further research in this evolving area is certainly needed; in the interim, it is fascinating to watch the evolution of cultural capital in its community development applications as Throsby's conceptions are tested and evaluated.

References

Bridger, Jeffrey C., and Theodore R. Alter. 2006. "Place, community development, and social capital." *Journal of the Community Development Society* 37:5–18.

Campbell, M. S. 1999. "New trends in cultural policy for the twenty-first century." *Social Text* 17:5–6.

Center for Arts and Culture. 2001. "America's cultural capital: Recommendations for structuring the federal role." *Journal of Arts Management, Law and Society* 31:180–83.

Cochrane, Phoebe. 2006. "Exploring cultural capital and its importance in sustainable development." *Ecological Economics* 57:318–330.

Creative City Network of Canada. 2008. *Cultural Sustainability/Cultural Capital.* Vancouver, B.C.: Creative City Network of Canada. Retrieved January 18, 2008. www.creativecity.ca/news/special-edition-4/key-contexts-2.html.

Department of Culture and the Arts. 2003. *Cultural Capital: A Sustainability Imperative.* Western Australia: Department of Culture and the Arts.

Emery, Mary, and Cornelia Flora. 2006. "Spiraling-up: Mapping community transformation with community capital framework." *Journal of the Community Development Society* 37:19–35.

Ginsburg, Victor, and David Throsby (eds.). 2006. *Handbook of the Economics of Art and Culture.* Amsterdam, The Netherlands: Elsevier North Holland.

Green, Gary Paul, and Anna Haines. 2007. *Asset Building and Community Development, 2nd Edition.* Thousand Oaks, CA: Sage Publications.

Jeannotte, Sharon. 2003. "Singing Alone? The contribution of cultural capital to social cohesion and sustainable communities." *The International Journal of Cultural Policy* 9: 35–49

Kretzmann, John P., and J. L. McKnight. 1993. *Building Communities from the Inside Out: A Path Toward Finding and Mobilizing a Community's Assets.* Evanston, IL: Center for Urban Affairs and Policy Research, Northwestern University.

Morato, A. R. 2003. "The culture society: A new place for the arts in the twenty-first century." *Journal of Arts Management, Law and Society* 32:245–256.

Phillips, Rhonda. 2002a. "Artful business: Using the arts for community economic development." *Community Development Journal* 39:112–122.

———. 2002b. *Concept Marketing for Communities.* Westport, CT: Praeger.

Radbourne, J., and Fraser, M. 1996. *Arts Management: A Practical Guide.* St Leonards, Australia: Allen and Unwin.

Shubik, M. 1999. "Culture and commerce." *Journal of Cultural Economics* 23:13–30.

Smith, Robert. 2000. "A success story: Bellows Falls praised for revitalization." *Eagle Times,* May 18, pp. B1, B3.

Throsby, David. 1994. "The production and consumption of the arts: A view of cultural economics." *Journal of Economic Literature* 32:1–29.

———. 1995. "Culture, economics and sustainability." *Journal of Cultural Economics* 19:199–206.

———. 2001. *Economics and Culture.* Cambridge, U.K.: Cambridge University Press.

UNESCO. 2001. Universal Declaration on Cultural Diversity. Paris, France: UNESCO.

World Commission on Culture and Development. 1996. *Our Creative Diversity*. Paris, France: Organization for Economic Co-operation and Development.

6 Neighborhood Approaches to Asset Mobilization

Building Chicago's West Side

JOHN P. KRETZMANN AND
DEBORAH PUNTENNEY

Introduction

I n a volume that explores asset-focused strategies for developing communities, few places could be a more appropriate source of rich examples than the City of Chicago. Its extraordinary history of community building and organizing—from Jane Addams through Saul Alinsky, the Civil Rights Movement, and today's wide variety of effective community development organizations—reflects the leading role Chicago has played in the invention of powerful neighborhood-based approaches to community improvement.

This chapter will highlight the asset-based strategies employed by two of the leading community development groups on Chicago's west side, the Westside Health Authority (WHA) and Bethel New Life. They are by no means the only effective groups working to improve Chicago's neighborhoods, but they exemplify those that consistently focus on the process of rediscovering and mobilizing the resources that are still present in their troubled communities.

A brief historical overview of Chicago's west side will help contextualize the work of WHA and Bethel New Life. These neighborhoods have exhibited the classic patterns of urban development in America over the past century and a half. Expanding out toward the prairie west of Chicago's downtown, they were home first to a variety of European working-class immigrants, including, in the first half of the twentieth century, the city's increasingly influential Jewish community. During and after the Second World War, the second wave of the Great Migration of African Americans spilled over the enforced racial boundaries of the south side of the city, and Blacks began to call the west side home.

Beginning in the 1950s, and accelerating through the 1960s and early 1970s, massive racial change transformed the west side of Chicago into an overwhelmingly African-American set of neighborhoods. As was the case in so many northern cities, the transformation was partly driven by real-estate practices that led to significant disinvestment on the west side by both the White residents who had previously occupied the neighborhoods and many of the institutions that served them. Blockbusting—sometimes referred to as panic peddling—was a tactic used by real-estate agents and speculators to realize substantial profits through manipulation of the racial makeup of specific community areas. These unscrupulous individuals triggered the turnover of White-owned property and homes to African Americans eager for housing outside of the overcrowded and impoverished south-side neighborhoods, using scare tactics that capitalized on existing racial tensions. Economic opportunity for the new residents was further reduced by the practice of redlining by financial institutions, which resulted in the gradual deterioration of west-side neighborhoods in the absence of capital for investment and redevelopment. Finally, a series of "riots"—the most extensive following the assassination of Dr. Martin Luther King Jr. in 1968—left many of the west side's commercial areas in ruins. During the accelerating decline over the next several years, more than 75 percent of the businesses in the community left the area. This included major industries like International Harvester, Sears, Zenith, Sunbeam, and Western Electric. By 1970, African Americans who could afford to do so were also leaving west-side communities like North Lawndale.

Today, the core west-side neighborhoods of East and West Garfield Park, Austin, and North Lawndale are still struggling to rebuild. The overwhelming majority of the population in these areas is African American (Austin has the lowest percentage of Blacks—almost 90 percent; West Garfield Park has the highest percentage—over 98 percent), with very small percentages of Whites and Hispanics residing there (from under 1 percent to just under 5 percent). East Garfield Park and Lawndale experienced a loss of population of more than 10 percent between the 1990 and 2000 census counts, and all of the west side suffers from higher-than-average crime rates and unemployment (U.S. Census 2000). The good news is that the struggle to rebuild in these areas is paying off. For example, *BusinessWeek* named East Garfield Park one of the country's "most up and coming neighborhoods" in 2007 (Rony 2007). Austin experienced a small increase in population during the 1990s. And the neighborhood organizations that emerged out of the struggles of the midcentury have made their presence known through locally based redevelopment efforts that have demonstrated success in terms of housing, jobs, and economic development, as well as infrastructure redevelopment.

Leading the rebuilding efforts is a group of remarkably feisty and creative community-based organizations. Among them are the Near West Side Community Development Corporation, the North Lawndale Christian Development Corporation, the South Austin Community Coalition, and the two we will profile in this chapter, Bethel New Life and WHA. Each of these organizations represents a case study in the kinds of positive things that can happen when communities commit to mobilizing local residents in community development efforts and to building on the assets they already possess.

Asset-Based Community Development in Action

For more than three decades, the Asset Based Community Development (ABCD) Institute at Northwestern University has worked with community builders in lower-income urban neighborhoods, including many in Chicago, to examine the dynamics of successful resident-driven development. These explorations led to a recognition and appreciation of the importance of local—or locally controlled—resources and their critical role in the most successful development efforts. These resources, or assets, constitute the fundamental material on which local development relies, and the term coined by the ABCD Institute, *asset-based community development*, describes the approach used in these communities. In fact, the Institute's research has consistently revealed the usefulness of anchoring community-driven development work in the combination of two or more of six basic categories of local assets. Present in every community, these six kinds of assets are the

- Skills, knowledge, and experience of local residents
- Power of local voluntary associations and networks of relationships
- Resources of local public, private, and nonprofit institutions
- Community's physical resources—for example, the land, buildings, and infrastructure
- Local economy—for example, producers, consumers, and barter and exchange activity
- Community's culture, history, and identity, particularly experiences of success

The ABCD Institute has come to understand successful, sustainable, resident-driven development as a set of processes involving the discovery ("mapping") of these assets, the building of connections and bonds among them, and the mobilization of these assets to accomplish useful projects and to advance a shared vision of the community's future. From a position of strength, then—as opposed to a plea for charity—a local community can build productive relationships both internally and with external entities like funders, government bodies, and technical-assistance providers. This "inside out" dynamic ensures that the community remains in control of the development processes and that investment in the community is focused on building on the positive elements of the community already identified rather than on negative depictions of the community and its needs (Kretzmann and McKnight 1993).

For both Bethel New Life and WHA, working with the neighborhood's assets is as natural as breathing. Bethel, growing out of a small Lutheran Church in West Garfield Park in the early 1980s, has leveraged community assets to build a $12-million-dollar-a-year multifaceted, community development corporation (McCullough 2008). WHA, created by local residents in the late 1980s, promotes its ambitious vision of a physically, economically, and socially healthy west side by mobilizing hundreds of volunteers, along with more than fifty staff members and a yearly budget of about $3.5 million (Reed 2008).

Both Bethel and WHA consistently engage all six categories of community assets in their efforts to improve the neighborhood. Their creative approaches to discovering, connecting, and mobilizing local resources have contributed significantly to the regeneration and renewal of the West Garfield Park and Austin neighborhoods. Following are some examples of their inventive strategies, organized around the six types of community assets.

Mobilizing the Skills, Knowledge, and Experience of Local Residents

Bethel and WHA anchor their community-building efforts in a commitment to the idea that every resident is a valuable human being. In language often heard in both organizations, every person is "a child of God." Interestingly, both groups have adopted the term *citizen leader* to define their aspirations for residents. In WHA, whose central community building strategy is called "Every Block a Village," each of sixty-eight blocks has selected a citizen leader, and these leaders define and help implement a community agenda at regular monthly meetings. For Bethel, identifying and training citizen leaders led to a series of small, very local community-building projects funded by minigrants. These minigrants supported projects such as community gardens and neighborhood beautification efforts that enable every local citizen to step forward and make a lasting contribution to his or her neighborhood.

As important as identifying and developing individuals into neighborhood leaders is that each organization places even more emphasis on strategies for reconnecting marginalized residents to the community and to the economy. Working with welfare recipients, homeless people, older adults, young people in trouble, ex-offenders, and the unemployed lies at the center of each group's mission. These efforts do more than reconnect people to community opportunities. Just as WHA and Bethel recognize that these individuals cannot live healthy lives if they are marginalized from the community, they also recognize that the community needs these residents in order to rebuild.

Mobilizing the Power of Local Associations and Networks of Relationships

Local associations represent the most important and powerful community-building asset there is because this is where residents and citizens come together voluntarily for the purpose of mutual enjoyment, effort, and experience. Early in our nation's history, local associations were one of the few sources of energy and commitment that could be applied to the task of building communities. Associations and the networks of relationships they represent are still a vitally important community-building resource. WHA and Bethel New Life are examples of organizations that understand the critical importance of local relationships—both existing associations and networks—as well as potential relationships among citizens. Faith-based organizations—in particular, the multiple versions of the African-American church—have been central building blocks for both organizations. WHA has worked with more than forty neighborhood organizations on a wide range of initiatives, while one of Bethel's predecessor organizations, Christian Action Ministry, was a multidenominational coalition of churches. In addition, both groups built upon the existing block clubs and immigrant associations, especially those based on relationships brought to the north by residents from small rural communities in Mississippi, Alabama, and other southern states. Building on existing associations and relationships has been an important strategy for both groups. But even more central to their success has been a commitment to strengthening local relationships and to creating new associational realities.

Some years ago, for example, Bethel leaders noticed that many unemployed residents, mostly women, were keeping busy providing care for older neighbors and relatives who were mostly homebound. Working with these "natural caregivers," Bethel negotiated with the state for the resources to start "In Home Care Services for the Elderly," a program designed to enable these caregivers to become formally employed in nursing positions. By bringing these women together and acknowledging their individual skills and capacities, Bethel launched an association of caregivers who encouraged one another to reach beyond their current caregiving roles. Bethel engaged the City of Chicago's community colleges to design a career ladder consisting of the training and ongoing education these women would need to transform their natural caregiving skills into paying jobs. Simultaneously, Bethel created local jobs in home health care, providing the opportunity for the newly credentialed nurse's aides to take up paid jobs in their own community, thus expanding their own well-being as they provided care to their neighbors. And the benefits of the program do not stop with the caregivers themselves. Among numerous success stories, Bethel founder and president emeritus Mary Nelson shares one about the forty-year-old woman who went back to school through the program and worked so hard that she altered the path of her entire family. As she struggled to prepare herself for a real job, her children, who might otherwise have chosen the life of the streets as so many young people do in Garfield Park, began to see her as a role model and began to shape their own school studies after her example.

Bethel's continuing commitments to the neighborhood's young people involve efforts like "Leading for Community Change," a youth-led visioning process that takes place in four local high schools. Once the young people have created their vision for the community, they develop action plans for implementing their collective visions, plans like the one for improving Madison Street, a central corridor through the neighborhood. In one project, young people who were formerly homeless partnered with senior citizens to design and build mosaics for public spaces in the community. Young and old people developed new sensitivities to their generational counterparts in this program, working together in ways that demonstrated their concern for fellow community members. For example, one older woman confined to a wheelchair could not normally have participated in such a building project, but the young people took the time to set up the mosaic construction so that she could position her chair close to the mosaic work and make a contribution to the project. One of the young men in this program had been living in a car, and the mosaic design that was used as the center of the project was his design. The impact on this young man of seeing his work as a central component of the public art piece was dramatic; he is completely changed by this experience. Where he had been withdrawn and isolated, he now is active in the high school and on the student council.

Another Bethel program, Welcome Home, helps address the difficulties associated with reintegrating the nearly four thousand ex-offenders who are released from prison into west-side communities each year. Bethel has fashioned the program to help ex-offenders establish positive relationships in the neighborhood and secure a stable economic future. This includes helping employers understand that they can be confident about hiring ex-offenders, as well as working with the ex-offenders to prepare them for employer expectations. For those who need to build an employment resume before they can obtain a regular job, Bethel offers internships that help these individuals develop work skills and demonstrate their reliability in a work setting.

Although Bethel New Life's community-building work does not emphasize the formation of voluntary groups as centrally as does WHA's Every Block a Village, they nonetheless are involved continuously in encouraging new block clubs, mutual support groups, and action-oriented resident groups related to education, economic development, housing, environmental sustainability, community history, and culture. Bethel has provided consistent leadership among faith-based groups on the west side, such as the West Side Isaiah Project, which produced sixty units of affordable housing. Both seniors and young people have been organized in a diverse array of voluntary activities, from the development of small businesses to a powerful series of efforts to recover and celebrate the community's history and cultural vitality.

WHA's commitments to integrating individual residents who are facing challenges into the larger community are equally evident. In WHA's core strategy, Every Block a Village, the most important responsibility of the citizen leader is to build ever-expanding social relationships on his or her block. Constantly looking for overlapping interests, gifts, concerns, and interests, citizen leaders convene small groups of neighbors to create a wide variety of new voluntary associations. This process, described by WHA founder and director Jackie Reed as "caring, sharing and giving among neighbors," has produced dozens of resident-defined associational groups. Many of the voluntary groups created by Every Block a Village extend WHA's commitment to promoting health, broadly understood. Local residents, not medical professionals, are assumed to be the primary producers of both individual and community well-being.

One of WHA's first efforts linked area hospitals and clinics with young people in local high schools to create a career ladder for nearly three hundred youth looking for pathways to secure adult employment. The effort drew the attention of the Chicago Public Schools, which then took over its management. Fresh Bread is a program that enables neighborhood people to reach out to youth and bring them into informal association within the broader community. Kids, their parents, and other neighborhood residents come to a local school on Saturdays; the teachers are there and everyone makes food, studies the Bible, or sometimes goes on a field trip. The young people—mostly boys—who have completed the program have all finished high school.

WHA also supports a program called the Freedom Riders, made up of a group of young people from the community learning what it takes to speak up and speak out about issues of importance in the community, especially education. At the block meetings that occur as part of Every Block a Village, local people talk regularly about the public schools and about their frustration with the schools' poor performance in educating the community's children. When WHA examined the schools via both a policy lens and a cultural lens, what it saw was young Black men being cast as the enemy, even within the schools they attend. WHA decided that local youth really needed to understand community activism in order to take on and lead the fight for better local schools themselves, and they modeled the program on the minority-led resistance efforts of forty years earlier—the Freedom Rides. WHA quickly discovered that it is not a problem getting kids to participate in the fight for a culture of learning in their community. The kids are enthusiastic about the opportunity to become activists on the issues that matter to them. They are now doing block-by-block recruiting for their Catch the Fever program, which involves five grammar schools actively helping to promote learning, and students are committing to a new way of approaching their studies. In the summer of 2007, the Freedom Riders campaigned for a new local school, and the group is now connected with the local park district, where their message reaches even more young people. The Freedom Riders have also organized a local teen center, doing all the painting and set-up work themselves. Having a tangible project like the teen center helps the young people develop their activism and prepare for both reactive and proactive endeavors on behalf of their community.

Other examples of WHA's commitment to bringing local people together in productive relationships include:

- A series of support groups, including those for grandparents and "caregivers"
- Kitchen Table, a group of local adults who come together to talk about losing weight, exercising, eating right, and stress relief
- Seniors on the Move, which has spawned a walking group, a choir, and a steppers group and is now using space at the neighborhood park

For both Bethel and WHA, the recognition of existing voluntary associations and networks along with the creation of new sets of relationships lie at the very center of their community-building commitments. Both Jackie Reed and Mary Nelson emphasize the critical importance of social capital and the enormous community development power expressed by citizens organized to work together.

Mobilizing the Resources of Local Public, Private, and Nonprofit Institutions

On the west side of Chicago, much of the important public institutional infrastructure—particularly the schools, parks, libraries, and transportation—has been allowed to deteriorate over the last forty years. In addition, many businesses abandoned the neighborhoods, while critical nonprofit institutions such as hospitals and clinics have been forced by economic challenges to close or relocate.

It is not surprising, then, that much of the attention of leading community development groups such as WHA and Bethel New Life has been focused on reinvigorating those institutions that remain and on creating new ones when possible. In particular, both Bethel and WHA have focused their energies on three priority institutional assets: schools, businesses, and health care.

In the 1980s, Ronald Reagan's secretary of education, William Bennett, famously labeled Chicago's public schools "the worst in the nation." Many local residents agreed. But since that time, school and political leaders have worked with parent and community groups to institute a series of school-reform initiatives. From a neighborhood perspective, the three most important changes involved (1) the creation of elected "local school councils," composed mainly of parents and community residents who were given authority to hire and fire the principal; (2) the assertion of accountability for low-performing schools, which provided new incentives for administrators; and (3) the city's move to replace the lowest-performing schools with small schools and charters. The first and third reform initiatives, in particular, opened the door for groups like WHA and Bethel to become significant players in relationship to their neighborhood schools. For example, both groups have actively recruited local residents and parents to run for seats on the local school councils and have helped provide training for council members. In addition, they have each worked to connect school curricula to employment opportunities in the health-care industry. And Bethel helped Flower High School fashion classroom approaches that built upon student-run enterprises, such as the Flower Pot Café and a school-based credit union. These efforts led to a community-wide Youth Enterprise Network that utilized the federal vocational education resources made available through the Carl Perkins Act to expand into three other area high schools. Bethel's continuing commitment to improving schools is expressed through its work with small schools and charters, including the Al Raby School, a high school whose highly experiential curriculum is founded on community and environmental studies.

The most successful community-building organizations focus on recognizing, retaining, and expanding their core community assets. In West Garfield Park and Austin, another critical set of local resources was represented by medical centers such as St. Anne's Hospital. When the religious order that owned St. Anne's announced its closing, the leaders of both Bethel and WHA rallied community support, raised funds, and put together an agreement leading to Bethel's ownership of St. Anne's campus (Snow 2001). What could have been a debilitating, abandoned eyesore in the center of the west side has been transformed into a multifaceted community asset. The Beth-Anne campus contains 186 units of senior citizen housing, a large day-care center, a job training facility, a theater-cultural complex, and a health clinic. Both WHA and Bethel continue to produce jobs and career ladders for residents interested in working in the health-care sector. WHA has been particularly successful in supporting and growing local businesses that sell needed supplies to hospitals and clinics.

Other important public institutional resources on Chicago's west side are the parks and libraries. Both WHA and Bethel have backed local parks by producing cooperative programming and resident support. And when the Legler Library—the regional library center for West Garfield and Austin—was threatened with closing, Bethel mobilized other community groups to come to its rescue. Their strategy focused on convincing the central library administration that the normal measures of a library's importance, such as the number of books circulated, might be less important than measures like the number of residents using the space. The strategy was successful. Bethel's reframing of the Legler Library as an institution occupying a central position in the community's health and well-being resulted in a beautifully renovated facility that serves the community in a variety of ways.

Powerful community-based nonprofits such as WHA and Bethel have now positioned themselves as valuable allies of institutions—public, private, and nonprofit—that are critical for the well-being of low-income neighborhoods. These groups, however, retain the autonomy to act as institutional critics when necessary. The ability to act in both roles—as partner and critic—appears to be important to the continuing revitalization of neighborhood institutions in low-income communities.

The Physical Resources of Local Communities

Driving through Chicago's west-side neighborhoods, one is still struck by the devastation that originated in the 1960s "riots" and persists to this day. Large strips of commercial properties have yet to be developed; many former industrial areas retain their toxic "brownfields" identity; and residential areas are pockmarked by vacant lots, many purged over time by arson-for-profit schemes. For WHA and Bethel New Life, restoring the neighborhoods' physical assets remains a central challenge. Both work on business retention and on the regeneration of schools and other public institutions.

In the past decade, Bethel has worked with other community groups to realize two highly significant victories for the physical assets of the neighborhood. First, Bethel was an important part of a coalition of city and suburban groups that successfully challenged the Chicago

Transit Authority's decision to close the Green Line, the elevated rapid-transit train that joined south-side, downtown, west-side, and west suburban travelers. This powerful community-driven effort not only saved the Green Line, but also ensured significant infrastructure improvements, including a modern new station at Lake Street and Pulaski Boulevard, which Bethel then used as the site for a new multifaceted green building.

In addition, Bethel was centrally involved in the successful campaign to restore one of the city's most significant public assets, the Garfield Park Conservatory. By the 1990s, the one-hundred-year-old conservatory that housed one of the largest collections of plants in the world had fallen into complete disrepair. Reflecting the broader withdrawal of infrastructure investment from this community, the potential for the total loss of the building mobilized local groups to action. After a winter freeze broke open the roofs and threatened the valuable vegetation, Bethel and an array of community allies began a political and financial campaign to restore the facility to the glory of designer Jens Jenson's original vision. It worked, and today the conservatory is a destination for more than 750,000 visitors each year.

New housing, revitalized public facilities, community parks and gardens, renewed public transportation—all of these restored physical assets generate hope among neighborhood residents and a willingness on the part of funders and government leaders to invest in the community's future.

Local Economic Resources

Both WHA and Bethel recognize two realities about their local economies. First, business abandonment and financial disinvestment over a number of years have had devastating effects. Second, significant skills, experience, networks, barter, and both small and large enterprises still remain. These realizations have led to a series of job training and employer-employee connection efforts, along with enterprise-creation strategies. Connections to the medical industry have been productive for both organizations, with job ladders being generated for both high school graduates and older residents with caregiving experience.

Bethel takes economic development seriously, but, like all its development efforts, emphasizes the needs of local people—regular people—as central to its economic activities. For example, the Community Savings Center offers community residents practical help with financial management, including the New Start Checking and the Smart Savers Program. The center offers classes, programs, and services for people who might be overlooked by more traditional banks, helping them understand and navigate such issues as predatory lending. Bethel has also established retail space for community-based, privately owned businesses, as well as community-based organizations, churches, and other groups with small-business ideas. By looking within the community to identify potential new business owners and serving them first of all, Bethel hopes to develop more resources, promote wealth creation, and encourage business retention in the neighborhood. Bethel is also involved in the development of housing and works with several partners on building affordable homes for local residents.

WHA also has an array of economic development initiatives, focusing especially on business development in the area of health. The $7.9 million Austin Wellness Center was completed in 2004 and serves as a catalyst for other development along the Chicago Avenue business corridor. The project was initiated by citizen leaders who were frustrated with the services provided by the County Medical Center in the community. Holding onto their vision for better local health care, the determined fund-raising efforts undertaken by these leaders helped make the new center a reality. Now the Wellness Center is anchored by several county health centers that cooperate in coordinating services to community residents. Working together, the community successfully ensured that more than half of the construction contracts associated with building the center were awarded to African-American contractors, and that 37 percent of them were neighborhood based. WHA is especially proud that the contractors involved were able to leverage their work on the Wellness Center to obtain larger construction contracts on nearby projects. A related project in the health industry has led WHA to foster local suppliers of medical goods to several health clinics in the community.

WHA also has a neighborhood-based Employment Center that emphasizes the building of community relationships and of employer trust as a key ingredient in the successful placement of local residents in jobs. The Employment Center goes beyond job placement by providing the kinds of support services—including assistance with housing, transportation, child care, and counseling—that help make obtaining and keeping a job possible. The Employment Center has successfully placed over seven hundred workers in permanent jobs.

Community Culture, History, and Success Stories

The final category of assets focuses on a community's identity—its values and culture, which constitute the stories that are shared about community pride and success. Both WHA and Bethel pay attention to the myriad cultural strengths of the west-side African-American communities. WHA devises community celebrations out of the rich history of the Civil Rights Movement. Bethel has sponsored a series of community-history explorations and celebrations that have drawn city-wide attention. Young people interviewed elders and produced an exhibition called "Looking Backward to Move Forward," which is now housed at the Harold Washington Library. Another intergenerational project produced "Journey from the Soles," an exhibit of shoes worn by west-side community heroes. The purposes of the exhibit are to pass along the tradition of community involvement and to challenge the next generation to be heroes in their own way. Many of these stories were transformed into a musical theater presentation, "Deep Enough to Swallow Me Whole," which featured more than sixty residents as cast members. In addition, young people and senior citizens have together created murals depicting neighborhood characters and events.

Obviously, the leaders of WHA and Bethel New Life understand that their neighborhoods face enormous challenges, including crime, unemployment, the lack of affordable housing, and struggling schools. Despite these daunting obstacles, these community builders continue to recognize the importance of focusing on the assets available for mobilization. No person is without gifts to contribute; no group of citizens can be ignored; no institution can be left on the sidelines; every physical, economic, and cultural asset is worth recognizing and involving.

Bethel's president and chief executive officer Steven McCullough speaks of creating a "Community of Choice" for the west side, a set of neighborhoods whose assets are so evident that people will choose to stay or move there. To reach that goal, Bethel, like WHA, focuses relentlessly not only on particular resources, but on the critical process of connecting those assets. Marginalized individuals are connected to existing associations or bonded to create new ones; public, private, and nonprofit institutions are brought into relationships with each other, as well as with local residents and their associations. Leaders consistently look to link existing and potential economic activity with the human and physical resources of the neighborhood. So the critical insight that guides the strategies of both WHA and Bethel is centered on the importance of relationships and on connecting the assets within the neighborhood.

The connected assets, then, represent the platform on which the neighborhood stands to speak to the variety of public and private resources outside the community. For the leaders of both Bethel and WHA, cultivating productive relationships with the leaders of those external institutions provides an ongoing set of challenges. The continuous courting of city, county, state, and federal elected officials, and of the relevant public-sector bureaucracies, is a high priority for both groups' leaders, and both go to great lengths to share credit with government partners for each accomplishment. They construct similar win-win relationships with supportive financial institutions and businesses, with religious institutions and other nonprofits, and with philanthropic organizations.

One central lesson has penetrated both groups—that is, every institution values the opportunity to be identified with success. When WHA and Bethel utilize the investments of major public, private, and philanthropic institutions to activate local residents; support the well-being of young people and families; create economic opportunities; and enhance the housing stock and improve the physical environment, the successes reflect positively on the wisdom of the investors and often lead to further productive relationships.

The central challenge for the community groups, particularly as their programs expand, is to retain control of their agendas. The leaders of Bethel and WHA seek to respond to both issues and opportunities defined at the community level, which are not necessarily the same as those articulated by funders and government agencies. Both Bethel and WHA try to pursue only those external resources that overlap significantly with their own locally defined priorities.

Another challenge facing successful community development groups involves the proliferation of program opportunities and the temptation to say "yes" to all of them. Bethel's Steven McCullough says, "We at Bethel simply can't do everything. So we are working to spin off some of our activities—for example, some of our cultural arts leadership. We need to focus our energies and resources on the core activities which we believe will create a 'community of choice.' For us, that means concentrating on jobs, housing and education" (Mc-Cullough 2008).

One final challenge faced by both WHA and Bethel has to do with the inherent tension between the values of professionalism and efficiency, on the one hand, and the critical commitment to participation and democratic decision making, on the other. As both groups have gotten larger and more complex, they have found and hired persons with valuable private-sector and managerial experience to lead their ambitious programs. Unlike the private sector, nonprofit community development groups strive to balance these perspectives with their deeply felt need to stay close to local residents and to construct useful methods that uncover resident concerns and mobilize their energies. WHA's Jackie Reed says, "We have lots of wonderful experts working with us now—many of them with roots in the community—but our real energies are still with the residents involved in Every Block a Village" (Reed 2008).

Given these challenges, WHA and Bethel invite not charity but rather investments from outside supporters. Balancing their cultivation of external assets with their mobilization of internal resources, they continue to attempt to turn their communities around. In effect, their message to governments and funders is, "We may not have all the resources we need, but we have located, connected, and mobilized all of the resources we do have. Now we invite your investment in our community's work."

This is a powerful recipe for building vital communities.

References

Kretzmann, John K., and John L. McKnight. 1993. *Building Communities from the Inside Out: A Path Toward Finding and Mobilizing a Community's Assets.* Evanston, IL: Institute for Policy Research, Northwestern University.

McCullough, Steven. 2008. Interview conducted on February 28 at Bethel New Life, Chicago, IL.

Reed, Jackie. 2008. Interview conducted on March 7 at Westside Health Authority, Chicago, IL.

Rony, Maya. 2007. "America's next hot neighborhoods." *BusinessWeek*, accessed on July 14, 2008. www.businessweek.com/bwdaily/dnflash/content/mar2007/db20070306_429975.htm?chan=search.

Snow, Luther. 2001. *Community Transformation: Turning Threats into Opportunities*. Evanston, IL.: Institute for Policy Research, Northwestern University.

U.S. Census. 2000. *Chicago Fact Finder*. Retrieved January 9, 2009, from Notre Dame University, Institute for Latino Studies Web site. www.nd.edu/~chifacts/chicago.html.

7 Natural Amenities and Asset-Based Development in Rural Communities

GARY PAUL GREEN

C ommunity assets can refer to the untapped skills, interests, and experiences of individuals; the potential social relationships embedded in community organizations; and the underutilized resources of local institutions. Asset-based development attempts to unlock these resources to benefit local residents (Kretzmann and McKnight 1993). Communities often begin the community development process by identifying problems or concerns—that is, performing a needs assessment. In many cases, needs assessments are conducted by outside organizers, consultants, or experts. Relying on external resources tends to incapacitate communities and makes them dependent on outsiders. Experts have limited understanding of the local resources that can enhance community capacity (Chaskin et al. 2001). Focusing on local problems and needs also tends to distract residents from opportunities and available resources. Asset-based development turns this approach on its head by identifying the resources that can enhance the community's quality of life.

The shift from needs assessment to asset building has been interpreted by some analysts as a move away from conflict to consensus organizing. Probably a more accurate characterization is that asset-based development provides the basis for a wider range of community-organizing tactics than is offered by needs assessment. Although conflict may eventually be a part of the strategy, asset-based development builds on values, visions, or both that are common across the community. Asset-based development also has been accused of focusing on local resources and excluding external influences on communities. The argument is frequently made that communities do not have the capacity or means to counter the larger economic, political, and social forces that shape communities today (Marwell 2007). Although asset-based development emphasizes the importance of local capabilities, it also stresses the necessity to leverage them to access external sources that are needed to promote development. Many poor communities need additional resources to implement their vision. But these resources should adapt to the vision, not the reverse. It also promotes the need to manage and control these resources locally.

Asset-based development usually begins with a mapping process that identifies individual skills, experiences, and interests. This process can be a valuable exercise because it documents the potential contributions of youth, retirees, and disabled residents. Each has the capacity to contribute to community well-being, yet they are often ignored in the community development process.

Most communities also have numerous formal and informal organizations. These organizations are potentially powerful actors in the development process because they hold social resources (relationships) that can facilitate collective action. Mapping the organizational terrain helps locate the levers for community change and the common values, interests, and goals that can serve as the basis for action. Many of the informal organizations, such as garden clubs and neighborhood watches, do not have any staff and are small in size. They can form, however, the building blocks for community development efforts (Ferguson and Dickens 1999).

Finally, local institutions (for instance, schools, hospitals, and libraries) have the potential of changing their policies and practices to better serve their community. For example, schools can change their purchasing patterns to support local businesses or their hiring practices to focus on the needs of local unemployed or underemployed workers. Hospitals can provide outreach to neighborhoods. Libraries can provide space for community meetings. These institutions are often limited by a bureaucratic ethos that has a minimal concern for the local environment in which they are located.

Once assets are mapped, it is possible for the community to develop a set of goals or a vision that will drive the development process. Mobilizing assets requires broad support among community organizations and institutions. The focus on local assets does not exclude accessing external resources. Local resources are leveraged to support community initiatives. This process also may involve a scan of allies and other potential sources of support that may be useful.

Much of the literature on asset-based development has focused on urban settings. An excellent example is the Dudley Street Neighborhood Initiative (DSNI) in Boston, which featured a grassroots approach to development that captured vacant property, held by absentee landlords, and used the land to build affordable housing and retail space (Medoff and Sklar 1994). The DSNI obtained the right of eminent domain from the city as part of its effort to manage their local resources. There has been much less research on asset-based development in rural areas. Differences between rural and urban communities are frequently overemphasized, but some important distinctions do remain. Rural communities are by definition smaller and often more socially isolated because of low levels of population density. They may lack social institutions that provide opportunities for interaction and social exchanges. The small size of many rural communities results in their often having limited resources.

Another fundamental difference between urban and rural communities, however, is the dependence on natural resources. In this chapter I focus on the role of natural resources in asset-based community development in rural communities. Dependency on natural resources historically has meant that the economies of rural areas are vulnerable to periods of boom and bust. This has especially been the case for many agricultural commodities, but also forestry and fishery products as well. Markets for these products can swing wildly, primarily because of changes in supply.

Management of natural resources is critical to the long-term sustainability of rural regions. One unique aspect of natural resources is that they tend to be multifunctional in nature (Knickel and Renting 2000). In other words, these resources can serve multiple functions and purposes. Historically, most natural resources have been viewed solely as commodities to be extracted for external markets (the production function). In many rural communities, these resources are now viewed as an amenity (the consumption function). In this chapter I discuss the role of natural amenities in asset-based development and examine a case study of a community heavily dependent on natural resources for its economic base.

Valuing Natural Resources

Natural resources typically play a pivotal role in the development of rural communities (Flora and Flora 2008). Historically, the economic base of rural communities has been deeply rooted in extractive industries, including agriculture, forestry, mining, and fishing. Natural resources have been viewed strictly as commodities to be sold to external markets. Some commodities are processed locally, so that much of the value added to the commodity is retained in the regional economy, while others are transported to other areas to be processed. Exports inject income and add jobs to the local economy both directly and indirectly through the purchase of additional goods and services.

Economic-development strategies based on a commodity approach to natural resources emphasizes promoting technological advancements and increasing economies of scale as means to generate jobs and income in rural communities. Unfortunately, these strategies lead to the substitution of capital for labor. This process has been most evident in the agricultural sector, but it is central to most other extractive industries as well. By viewing natural resources as commodities, economic development typically results in great competition and, ultimately, increased productivity as a means of survival.

These economic-development strategies have been criticized heavily. One of the major criticisms is that increased competition contributes to greater concentration and centralization of production. Because of economies of scale, large producers drive out smaller producers. Dependency on natural resources leads to large swings in the economy because these commodities are vulnerable to large shifts in supply. Increasingly, critics have charged that these economic-development strategies are not sustainable. This model of economic development produces environmental problems and risks (Schnaiberg 1980). Commodity production and concentration of production in agriculture tend to rely on increased use of chemical inputs, soil erosion, and pollution. Similarly, commodity production in other industries, such as fishing and forestry, can lead to overproduction and scarcities without regulation.

There is a growing recognition that natural resources have an economic value that is frequently ignored by rural (and urban) residents. The amenity value of natural resources often exceeds the commodity value (Power 1996). Amenities are nonmarketed qualities of a community that make it an attractive place to live, work, or visit (Green 2001). Amenity-led development has played a critical role in the rapid population and employment growth in the U.S. South and West during the 1980s and 1990s. Many of these regions that have experienced the most growth were in the mountains and on the coasts. Natural amenities, however, go beyond mountains and oceans. The concept also includes lakes and rivers, landscapes, cultural attractions, forests, and even the small-town atmosphere in rural areas. In most cases, natural amenities are fixed—they cannot be created or moved, and once they are gone they cannot be recreated.

As I have indicated, natural amenities have been a key source of growth in the Mountain West and the South over the past twenty-five years. David McGranahan (1999) has demonstrated how climate was strongly related to rural population change in the 1980s and 1990s. Proximity to water has also been a major factor in this migration pattern (Goe and Green 2005). Much of the economy in amenity communities is related to tourism and recreation (Johnson and Beale 2002). In some communities, tourists are attracted on a relatively short-term basis. Other communities are able to draw seasonal residents who are attracted to the natural amenities in the region. Rural areas in relatively close proximity to urban areas have been more likely to develop as tourist destinations and as sites for seasonal home development (Green, Deller, and Marcouiller 2005). Another important foundation of amenity-based development over the past few decades has been migration among retirees. Retirees also have been attracted to communities that have protected and managed their natural resources.

Natural amenities are highly elastic, which means that as income rises they are more valued. The economic expansion of the 1990s fueled the higher demand for living in high-amenity areas (Green and Clendenning 2003). This expansion included not only migrants to amenity areas, but also seasonal residents and tourists.

The value of natural amenities can be shaped by a variety of factors. One source of amenity value is *use value*. Individuals derive benefits from direct physical use of these resources, such as is the case in recreation and tourism. In some instances, users pay a fee that makes it possible to attach a value to these amenities. In other cases, the amenities are public goods. This means that consumers of natural amenities may not be paying the full cost of maintaining the amenity (free-riding). For example, urban residents who drive out to rural areas to enjoy the fall colors generally do not pay for the benefits they derive from the landscape. Rural residents often subsidize this type of tourism. Presumably there is some economic benefit, however, as tourists spend money while visiting the area. Economists have developed methodological tools to estimate the public's willingness to pay for public goods through taxes. But it is difficult to tax many of the users of amenities because they may not reside in the region.

Individuals do not have to use an amenity to derive some value or benefit from it. There are three alternative reasons why individuals may value an amenity they are not using. First, they may not intend to use the amenity now, but want to keep the option available to use it in the future (*option value*). Individuals may be willing to pay taxes for parks and recreation areas with the idea that they will visit these areas sometime in the future and receive some benefits from it.

Second, some individuals may prize the simple existence of an amenity (*existence value*). For example, many people may appreciate the preservation of natural areas in Alaska, although few actually plan to visit the area. In many cases, individuals are willing to tax themselves to insure that these natural areas remain intact. Economic tools have a more difficult time capturing the value of these amenities because it is based more in individual beliefs than actual behavior.

Third, individuals may wish to pass on the amenities to future generations (*bequest value*). They may not use it themselves, but they are satisfied to leave it to future generations for their use.

Research on the outcomes and impacts of amenity-based development is somewhat mixed. Amenity-based development contributes to income growth in rural areas, but has a negligible effect on income inequality and poverty (Green, Deller, and Marcouiller 2005). Jobs in the tourist industries tend to be low-wage and often seasonal in nature (Becker and Bradbury 1994). Although jobs and income are being created, there tend to be few middle-class jobs for residents (Leatherman and Marcouiller 1999).

In many amenity areas, communities struggle with providing affordable housing for service-sector workers. The fiscal demands of building and maintaining the physical infrastructure for tourism can be overwhelming for many local governments (Deller, Marcouiller, and Green 1997). Amenity-based development also may fail to manage growth that potentially could destroy the quality of life that attracts new residents and visitors. There is considerable debate over the appropriate governmental level at which natural amenities should be managed. Eric Olson (2005) argues that natural resource protection should take place at the local level, while others have called for a regional approach (Daniels 1999).

This brief review suggests that there are several challenges for communities seeking to promote asset-based development in rural areas. First, how do rural communities manage the conflict between residents seeking to promote the amenity value versus the commodity value of natural resources? Second, can rural communities avoid many of the weaknesses of amenity-based development, such as seasonal and low-wage work and high taxes, to maintain the infrastructure? And finally, is it possible to maintain a multifunctional environment in these settings? In other words, can communities continue to support commodity agriculture and forestry while simultaneously promoting tourism and residential development?

In the following paragraphs, I present a case study that examines the role of natural amenities in a tourist destination—Petoskey, Michigan. I conducted focus groups with business leaders, government officials, seasonal residents, and full-time residents in the region. The discussion centered on the development in and the consequences for various populations in the region. I explore several issues in this case study. First, I am interested in the potential conflicts between tourists (and seasonal residents) and full-time residents over the nature of development in the region. Second, I assess some of the implications of amenity-based development for the region. Finally, I examine some of the issues in managing growth and development in a natural amenity region.

Natural Amenities in Petoskey, Michigan

Northern Michigan has been a relatively poor region that historically has been dependent on its natural resources as a major source of income. Until the 1950s, most of the region's economy was based on forestry (especially pulp logging and wood chipping) and agricultural production (Rathge and Beegle 1985; Schwarzweller and Lean 1993). In the 1950s, mining (limestone, dolomite, gypsum, rock salt, brine, sand, and gravel) provided a major source of employment in northern Michigan, putting more than thirteen thousand people to work. Some of the minerals were processed locally (such as limestone and gypsum at cement plants in Alpena and Petoskey), but most were shipped to builders elsewhere in the Midwest (Strassman 1958).

Over the past fifty years, tourism has risen in economic importance in the region. Although much of the growth in tourism is fairly recent, the area has a long history of attracting urban residents. The tourism industry is built around the needs and interests of wealthy seasonal residents. Wealthy Detroit industrialists and their families have vacationed in Petoskey and Charlevoix since the beginning of the twentieth century. Petoskey is well known for being the site of Ernest Hemingway's summer home. In 1919, Hemingway moved to Petoskey and wrote the *Torrents of Spring*, which features several Petoskey locations, such as Brown's Beanery (which was based on Braun's Restaurant). The growth of the resort industry, mostly built on skiing and snowmobiling, is seen as complementing tourism and making the region more attractive in the winter. The growth in number of seasonal homes in the region has had an important impact on the expansion of the construction industry and the health-care industry.

Since the railroad connected to Petoskey in 1890, the area has been a fashionable summer resort. The community originated as a Methodist summer retreat offering intellectual and cultural programs. The Chautauqua-like atmosphere has been maintained by the contemporary Bay View Association, which organizes an annual Chautauqua filled with seminars, lectures, a music festival, productions of Broadway plays, and even an opera.

The Petoskey region is known throughout the Midwest for its large stock of Victorian homes. The area has the largest collection of historic homes in the country, with 440 Victorian homes on the National Historic Register. These Bayview homes are not winterized, and the land beneath them is owned by the railroad. In part because of this unusual land tenure system, and justified as a way to prevent fires from area heaters, most of the Victorian homes are abandoned after October 31 as the railroad does not permit residents in the homes after this date.

The addition of skiing resorts in the region has increased the number of tourists who visit the area in the winter months as well. In the winter, the area receives an average of 121 inches of snowfall, and it is estimated that about a quarter-million skiers stay overnight in the area from November to March. As I will discuss subsequently, the winter tourism industry has had a significant impact on the overall development process in the region. In the past, seasonal residents closed their houses in the fall and returned in the spring. Today, many seasonal residents and tourists continue to visit the area throughout the year. This has had the effect of extending the seasonal employment in the region.

One of the most significant development projects in the region was the 1995 opening of the Bay Harbor Golf Club. This is a private club with memberships that were selling for more than $25,000 apiece. The course is located along a four-kilometer stretch of cliffs that plunge hundreds of feet down to Lake Michigan's Little Traverse Bay (Cantor 1997). It was built on an abandoned quarry and cement plant where waste from the limestone processing had seeped into the lake. Only a legal reconstruction of property rights (the Michigan Environmental Response Act, which protects a developer from lawsuits related to the redevelopment of derelict property) made the site affordable for redevelopment. David V. Johnson not only bought the Bay Harbor development site, but in addition owns most of the South Fox Island in northern Lake Michigan.

Bay Harbor also built 850 residential units. Bay Harbor has received support from many local residents because it helped them solve their water problems. The city of Petoskey was under an Environmental Protection Agency order to find new wells or go out into Lake Michigan and build a new intake system, which would have cost about $10 million. Instead, four fresh-water wells were found in the development, and it now supplies enough water for the city. The town has formally annexed Bay Harbor.

Petoskey has a strong historic preservation program and is concerned with managing the growth that occurs in the region. Both Charlevoix and Petoskey, which are the trade centers of the region, have done impressive jobs of preserving the historic nature of their downtown areas. Both areas remain economically vibrant; this adds to the charm of the communities. Shopping in these areas, however, is generally oriented toward high-income consumers, with plenty of exclusive clothiers, art galleries, and jewelry stores. One sign of the protectionist interests and collective action of the residential, business, and resort communities is an extended battle to prevent Wal-Mart from building a store in Petoskey. In 1994, representatives of RG Enterprises of Dayton, Ohio, presented to the Bear Creek Township Planning Committee their plan to build a strip mall on eighty-seven acres of land off U.S. Highway 131, two miles south of downtown Petoskey. The mall would have been anchored by a 130,000-square-foot Wal-Mart and a 65,000-square-foot Elder-Beerman, a nondiscount department store similar to Hudson's. The township approved the plan, and opponents took them to court to stop the project. After a fairly extensive litigation process, the courts decided in favor of the township. RG Properties began construction in May 1996. Wal-Mart opened for business in January 1997. The Elder-Beerman store was never built because the company declared bankruptcy and an Office Max was built instead.

Several changes may affect the development in the region. One of the most important is a new U.S. 31 bypass, which will be built to cope with heavier traffic in the area. This development project will inevitably have a large economic impact on the area and threatens its image as a historic and small-town location. The debate centers on where the bypass will be located and whether it should be built anew or use existing roads.

The growth of the resort industry has been a driving economic force in the region. Several issues contributed to the rapid development of this industry. First, many Petoskey business leaders reported that the increasing wealth of the upper middle class, due especially to the stock market rises of the 1990s, have made it possible for more people to own seasonal homes, and the Petoskey region is an attractive site for these homes. Some people who had made large gains in the stock market were looking to find places to invest that had very little risk, and seasonal homes appeared to be a logical place to invest.

Many of these people were buying second homes outside of Petoskey—around the many lakes in the region. Several of the Petoskey business leaders discussed how the growth of seasonal homes in the area had driven up housing costs and property taxes, making it more difficult for local residents to find affordable housing.

Second, the development of ski and golf recreation in the region has added jobs and income to the regional economy. Ski resorts have attracted tourists during the winter and created new demand for hotels. Golf courses also have attracted a different type of tourist than the seasonal resident.

Third, many of the business leaders attributed much of the success in Petoskey to the Bay View Association, which had been active in promoting historic preservation. Thus far, Petoskey has avoided some of the negative consequences (for example, traffic congestion) of tourist development that were evident in nearby Traverse City. Everyone agreed that Traverse City was a good example of what to avoid.

All of the seasonal residents I interviewed expressed concern with the rapid growth that had occurred in the region. They had several different types of complaints. Traffic and congestion were probably the most important concerns. In Petoskey, there is one major highway that runs north-south through the city. In the summer, the traffic is heavy, and most local residents avoid going through that part of town if they can. A related theme was the concern with land-use issues in the region. The focus group participants emphasized there are strong lakes associations in the area, but the towns are not working well together. Most of the seasonal residents are in favor of more controls to land use and growth management in general. Another concern among seasonal residents is with the population pressure on the lakes in the region. Long-term seasonal residents were especially perturbed by the number of boaters and jet skis on many of the lakes today.

Petoskey struggles to maintain the amenities that have made it an attractive place to live and work. Residents (both full- and part-time) believe the city must manage growth and development in the region so as to preserve the quality of life. They often point to other tourist destinations in the region that have not been able to adequately control growth.

One of the most important developments in recent years has been the rise of the skiing industry, which has promoted year-round tourism. In the past, many workers in northern Michigan would rely on unemployment or welfare payments to help support themselves during the winter months. Historically, hunting and fishing also provided a supplemental source of income during the winter. The availability of jobs through most of the year has increased consumer spending in the region and added more jobs to the economy. Many of the seasonal residents also now have winterized their homes and spend more time in the area during the winter.

Expansion of the health-care industry has had a major impact on the region's economy. Growth in the number of retirees in the region has increased substantially the demand for health-care services. In turn, access to excellent health care has served as an important attraction for retirees. The health-care industry has provided stable, well-paying jobs. Similarly, the construction industry had a significant impact, but that effect will probably not continue over the long run.

Conclusions

Asset-based development emphasizes mapping, controlling, and leveraging local resources. Local resources are managed to minimize dependencies and to maximize benefits for residents of the community. Rural communities present some rather unique challenges to promoting asset-based development. They often lack control over many of their resources, and the population density and size make it difficult to mobilize resources. Natural resources continue to be a critical asset for rural communities. Once destroyed, natural resources are difficult to replace or replenish. They are multifunctional resources that can serve several purposes. The case of Petoskey, Michigan demonstrates how a rural region has successfully made the transformation from relying on natural resources as extractive industries to relying on them as natural amenities.

Most of the discussion in this chapter has focused on how assets can contribute to economic development. It should be recognized that the relationships between natural and cultural assets and economic development can be quite precarious. On the one hand, preserving or enhancing natural, and cultural, assets may require a minimal level of economic development. Establishing a natural area for an ecotourism project may require an investment in land as well as infrastructure support. Maintaining a historic downtown area may necessitate public (government) expenditures or incentives.

On the other hand, nature is a unique resource that needs to be managed carefully in the economic-development process. Rapid growth can diminish the current or future value of these assets. Once destroyed, they cannot be easily replaced or reproduced. In areas dependent on tourism, additional traffic, construction, and population growth may diminish the use value associated with resources. Petoskey residents appreciated the importance of their local efforts and sought to manage them in a way that preserved them for the future.

There are some systematic differences, however, in the growth-management values and goals of seasonal and permanent residents. Full-time residents are more likely to favor more growth and development, while seasonal residents typically support less growth and development. There may be several reasons for these differences. Seasonal residents tend to be wealthier than full-time residents. Thus, they may be able to pay higher taxes. Full-time residents are more likely to be concerned with creating job opportunities for family members and increasing the tax base in the community. Full-time residents are more likely to have political power in the community unless seasonal residents can organize themselves and become engaged in the political process.

Natural amenities potentially serve the interests of nonlocal consumers. They can be public goods, which means that consumers cannot be excluded and it is difficult to compensate communities for the costs of maintaining and preserving these assets. Rural communities are often faced with the financial responsibility for maintaining the natural amenities, while urban residents are the primary beneficiaries. There may be several strategies to pay for these public goods. The most common strategy would be to tax all residents, both urban and rural, in order to pay for these amenities. Another approach is to tax just the users, which is possible only in areas where use can be restricted.

Another component of local control of natural amenities concerns the ownership patterns among businesses. Many firms exploiting natural resources in extractive industries tend to be owned and controlled by outside interests. The large timber companies that owned much of the land in the northern Michigan are an example. Although some of the recent development in the region is based on outside resources, it appears that asset-based development of natural amenities relies heavily on local investments and interests.

There are a few lessons from this case study for community development practitioners. Amenity-based development can be a challenge because of different interests among residents regarding economic growth. Petoskey was successful because residents recognized that historic preservation and management of natural amenities can contribute to economic development. Framing the issue in this manner helped overcome some of the potential conflicts between residents wanting more economic growth and those more concerned with preserving the environment.

Amenity-based development in this region was successful for a couple of other reasons. The community was able to avoid the "tourism trap" by finding ways of promoting year-round job opportunities. Recreation based on skiing and snowmobiling has opened up a different economy of residents in the region. As a result, income has risen and job opportunities have increased. Another important aspect of the community's strategy has been to diversify its economy. Growth of the health-care sector has been especially important in this regard. Not only has the health-care industry provided good middle-class jobs, it has supported the retirement sector. Older residents will be attracted to the region because of the quality health care that can be provided.

References

Becker, Barbara, and Susan L. Bradbury. 1994. "Feedback on tourism and community development: The downside of a booming tourist economy." *Journal of the Community Development Society* 29:268–276.

Cantor, George. 1997. "Michigan's northern exposure." *The Detroit News*, June 1, B4.

Chaskin, Robert J., Prudence Brown, Sudhir Venkatesh, and Avis Vidal. 2001. *Building Community Capacity*. New York: Walter de Gruyter.

Daniels, Thomas. 1999. *When City and Country Collide: Managing Growth on the Metropolitan Fringe*. Washington, DC: Island Press.

Deller, Steven C., David W. Marcouiller, and Gary P. Green. 1997. "The influence of recreational housing development on local government finances." *Annals of Tourism Research* 24:1–28.

Ferguson, Ronald F., and William T. Dickens (Eds.). 1999. *Urban Problems and Community Development*. Washington, DC: Brookings Institute Press.

Flora, Cornelia Butler, and Jan L. Flora. 2008. *Rural Communities: Legacy and Change*, 3rd Edition. Boulder, CO: Westview Press.

Goe, W. Richard, and Gary Paul Green. 2005. "Amenities and change in the well-being of nonmetropolitan localities." Pp. 95–112 in *Amenities and Rural Development: Theory, Methods, and Public Policy*, edited by Gary Paul Green, Steven C. Deller, and David W. Marcouiller. Cheltenham, U.K. and Northhampton, MA: Edward Elgar Publishing.

Green, Gary Paul. 2001. "Amenities and community economic development." *Journal of Regional Analysis and Policy* 31:61–76.

Green, Gary Paul, and Greg Clendenning. 2003. "Seasonal homes." Pp. 1210–1213 in *Encyclopedia of Community*, edited by Karen Christensen and David Levinson. Thousand Oaks, CA: Sage Publications.

Green, Gary Paul, Steven C. Deller, and David W. Marcouiller (Eds.). 2005. *Amenities and Rural Development: Theory, Methods, and Public Policy*. Cheltenham, U.K. and Northhampton, MA: Edward Elgar Publishing.

Johnson, Ken M., and Calvin L. Beale. 2002. "Nonmetro recreation counties: Their identification and rapid growth." *Rural America* 17:12–19.

Knickel, K., and H. Renting. 2000. "Methodological and conceptual issues in the study of multifunctionality and rural development." *Sociologia Ruralis* 40:512–528.

Kretzmann, John P., and John L. McKnight. 1993. *Building Communities from the Inside Out: A Path Toward Finding and Mobilizing a Community's Assets*. Evanston, IL: Center for Urban Affairs and Policy Research, Northwestern University.

Leatherman, John, and David W. Marcouiller. 1999. "Income distribution characteristics of rural economic sectors: Implications for local development policy." *Growth and Change* 27:434–459.

Marwell, Nicole P. 2007. *Bargaining for Brooklyn: Community Organizations in the Entrepreneurial City*. Chicago, IL: University of Chicago Press.

McGranahan, David A. 1999. *Natural Amenities Drive Rural Population Change*. Agricultural Economic Report No. 781. Washington, DC: Food and Rural Economics Division, Economic Research Service, U.S. Department of Agriculture.

Medoff, Peter, and Holly Sklar. 1994. *Streets of Hope: The Fall and Rise of an Urban Neighborhood*. Boston, MA: South End Press.

Olson, Eric. 2005. "Raising the gangplank: A defense of localism aimed at resource protection." Pp. 282–301 in *Amenities and Rural Development: Theory, Methods, and Public Policy*, edited by Gary Paul Green, Steven C. Deller, and David W. Marcouiller. Cheltenham, U.K. and Northhampton, MA: Edward Elgar Publishing.

Power, Thomas Michael. 1996. *Lost Landscapes and Failed Economies: The Search for a Value of Place*. Washington, DC: Island Press.

Rathge, Richard W., and J. Allan Beegle. 1985. "The consequences of population growth for pine tree country, Michigan." Pp. 69–90 in *Research in Rural Sociology and Development,* vol. 2, edited by Frank A. Fear and Harry K. Schwarzweller. Greenwich, CT: JAI Press.

Schnaiberg, Allan. 1980. *The Environment: From Surplus to Scarcity.* New York: Oxford University Press.

Schwarzweller, Harry K., and Sue-Wen Lean. 1993. "Ontonagon: A remote corner of Michigan's Upper Peninsula." Pp. 168–194 in *Forgotten Places: Uneven Development in Rural America,* edited by Thomas A. Lyson and William W. Falk. Lawrence: University of Kansas Press.

Strassman, W. Paul. 1958. *Economic Growth in Northern Michigan: Trends in Tourism, Agriculture, Mining and Manufacturing.* East Lansing: Michigan State University.

8 Implementing Community Development in the Mississippi Delta

The Effect of Organizations on Resident Participation

MARK H. HARVEY AND
LIONEL J. BEAULIEU

Introduction

For more than four decades, community-based initiatives to develop distressed areas have achieved limited success (Clark, Southern, and Beer 2007; Giloth and Dewitt 1995; Green and Haines 2002; Richards and Dalbey 2006). With few exceptions (see Medoff and Sklar 1994), the goal of building the leadership skills of a new cadre of local residents and empowering them to become more active players in community-improvement activities has proved to be more of a pipe dream than a reality. Too often, such programs have failed to garner participation beyond the usual suspects—local power brokers and community-based nonprofit organizations (such as community development corporations, or CDCs) that are attracted to these initiatives in hopes of securing funds that can be used to support their own particular goals (Hayward, Simpson, and Wood 2004; Hickey and Mohan 2005; McAreavey 2006; Shucksmith 2000). As a result, the work of attending to the "big picture" issues facing communities—such as upgrading local educational systems, improving access to health care, generating well-paying jobs, increasing inventories of affordable housing, and creating safe neighborhoods—is rarely pursued with the full spectrum of local voices at the table, and even more rarely achieved.

An unfortunate outgrowth of the limited progress made toward tackling the pervasive problems facing distressed places is that those most capable of creating change have opted to leave, migrating to places where job opportunities and quality of life are better (Lehmann 1991; Wilson 1987). As such, distressed communities (urban as well as rural) have witnessed an ongoing erosion of their middle classes that has reduced the numbers of residents with the skills, experiences, and resources needed to lead efforts aimed at improving the long-term viability of the communities.

Recent literature assessing community development initiatives that place local residents in leadership roles highlights the difficulties associated with bringing together diverse groups of citizens to work in partnership with professional and community-based organizations to identify priority issues and develop and implement plans for change (Aigner, Flora, and Hernandez 2001; Austin 2000; Green and Haines 2002; Kubisch et al. 2002; Pavey et al. 2007; Schafft and Greenwood 2003; Sojourner et al. 2004). Even more difficult is the challenge of engaging low-wealth residents in such processes in meaningful ways (Fagotto and Fung 2006; Parisi et al. 2002). This presents a substantial problem for community development initiatives targeting high-poverty communities. The literature indicates that garnering the participation of low-wealth residents requires the leadership of a highly resourced and professionalized organization—in other words, a strong organization (Fagotto and Fung 2006; Kubisch et al. 2002; Stoecker 1997).

This chapter extends the research on the relationship between professional implementing organizations and resident participation by conducting an in-depth examination of community development initiatives spearheaded by two different types of organizations in one of the nation's most impoverished regions, the Mississippi Delta. One organization, a regional philanthropic foundation, implemented an initiative based on grassroots resident empowerment in two noncontiguous Delta counties. The other, a community development financial institution (CDFI), took a more professionally managed top-down approach in which its efforts were highly concentrated in the economic hub of the one county in which it chose to work.

Our monitoring of these organizations and their approaches allows us to address a number of questions of interest to community development scholars and practitioners: (1) What barriers within high-poverty communities block or limit the success of resident-driven initiatives? (2) What are the strengths and weaknesses of different types of professional organizations in terms of overcoming these barriers? (3) How do organizational strengths and weaknesses interact with community conditions to facilitate or inhibit progress? (4) To what extent does the ethic of citizen control (Arnstein 1969), a key component of the asset-based approach (see Green and Haines 2002), facilitate or detract from the attainment of meaningful change?

Our findings are somewhat counterintuitive in that the organization that implemented a highly centralized and professionalized approach achieved more success in building a foundation for long-term resident-driven community transformation than the organization expressly dedicated to grassroots control. This finding lends support to scholars who question the effectiveness of approaches that posit a zero-sum relationship between professionalization and resident participation (Boyle and Silver 2005; Schafft and Greenwood 2003; Stoecker 1997). It also lends support to scholars who argue that community development initiatives would be more effective if stronger organizations displaced the small ones with weak resources, such as local CDCs, that usually lead local implementation processes (Fagotto and Fung 2006; Kubisch et al. 2002; Stoecker 1997). Additionally, the findings support the argument that implementing organizations working in highly distressed places that are plagued by deep-rooted social conflict—for example, the racial divide in the Mississippi Delta—would benefit from abandoning the role of detached facilitator of communication and assuming that of an actively engaged negotiator of conflict (Leeuwis 2000; see also Sojourner et al. 2004).

The remainder of the chapter is organized as follows: First, we provide a review of the literature on resident participation in community development initiatives, paying special attention to professionalization and organizations. Next, we provide an overview of the methodological approach we used in evaluating the two initiatives. We then present our findings, beginning with a description of the obstacles to resident-led community development in the Delta. This is followed by descriptions of our two cases, focusing on key differences in (1) organizational characteristics and capacities, (2) approaches to resident participation, and (3) how those approaches and characteristics interacted with local conditions. Next, we present interview data documenting resident participants' and nonparticipants' experiences with and perceptions of each initiative. We conclude with a discussion of the implications of our findings for community development theory and practice in highly distressed places like the Delta. We concur with those who have called for greater professionalization carried out by stronger organizations with the capacity to play a strategic role in negotiating conflict. We also discuss the potential problems associated with such an approach.

Resident Participation and Professional Organizations

The ideal of resident participation in decision-making processes is at the heart of democratic theory and holds a privileged position in the political and civic traditions of the United States (Tocqueville (1835)). It also holds a privileged position in the theory and practice of community development, including the asset-based community development approach (Green and Haines 2002). Since its emergence in the1950s, the field of community development has emphasized resident participation in decision making and leadership (Arnstein 1969; Voth 1975). From a normative perspective, resident participation is an end in itself. From an instrumental standpoint, the knowledge, skills, and energy that resident participants bring to initiatives are seen as invaluable to the achievement of meaningful outcomes (Gittell 1980; Hardina 2006; Stoecker 1997). Noting that resident participation can take many forms, Schafft and Greenwood (2003:19–20) offer a loose definition: "The inclusion of a diverse range of stakeholder contributions in an ongoing . . . process from the identification of problem areas to the development, implementation and management of strategic planning."

From Participatory to Professionally Led Community Development

The historical roots of community development in the United States evidence a philosophy that held grassroots leadership to be foundational. President Lyndon B. Johnson's Community Action Program (CAP) of

1965, for example, sought to revitalize distressed places by empowering and mobilizing low-wealth residents to take control of their communities. In this context, participation reflected a belief that beneficiaries should play a central role in designing and administering the programs intended to help them. Thus, during the early years of CAP, grassroots leaders were given control over federal funds to create programs to address resident needs. As it happened, leaders also used program resources to mobilize residents, challenging the authority of entrenched political elites (Orleck 2006; Quadagno 1994). Although this approach achieved some important successes, it was limited by residents' lack of access to capital and limited technical skills. Moreover, the challenges posed to local elites provoked powerful opposition that undermined the achievement of broader community-wide effects (Orleck 2006).

Within a short time, however, a more top-down, professionally driven model emerged as the dominant approach. The key actors were local organizations staffed by community development professionals who delivered government and philanthropically funded services to residents of low-income communities. Evidence of this shift is reflected in the massive proliferation of CDCs during the 1970s (Krumholz et al. 2006; Stoecker 1997). Although claiming to reflect the ideal of citizen control, over time the CDC model effectively eliminated residents from active participation in decision-making processes, relegating them to membership on oversight boards to which professional staff would periodically report (Clark, Southern, and Beer 2007; Richards and Dalbey 2006).

At the same time, federal funding for community development was attracting other entities, such as municipalities and developers, into the field, resulting in the development of what Yin (1998) calls the "community development industry system" (CDIS). According to Yin, the CDIS comprises formal and informal organizations with an interest in community development. These include CDCs as well as a variety of other "local participants, such as corporations, local government, neighborhood interests, and for-profit developers" and a variety of "extra local participants, such as the federal government, national foundations, and national organizations" (Yin 1998:138).

In high-poverty rural areas, where jobs and resources for development are scarce, the CDIS developed into a pillar of local economies (Duncan 1999; Lehmann 1991). As such, in these areas the CDIS is marked less by cooperation among organizations than by fierce competition. The literature shows that CDIS organizations tend to prefer to function as silos rather than work together to tackle community problems, and that they are highly protective of their turf (Aigner, Flora, and Hernancez 2001; Clark, Southern, and Beer 2007; Frisch and Servon 2006; Giloth and Dewitt 1995). They are also often enmeshed in patronage politics. In sum, the function of the CDIS in many rural areas has been to militate against community-oriented behavior by entities charged with community development (Cobb 1992; Duncan 1999; Lehmann 1991).

The Rise of Community Development Financial Institutions

While the CDC model continues to play a leading role in community development, it faces new competition from an emergent, market-oriented approach in which CDFIs play the lead role. CDFIs are nonprofit subsidiaries of bank holding companies that are chartered, under the Community Reinvestment Act, to do community development lending (Curtis 2006). The CDFI approach sees lack of access to capital as the main problem facing economically distressed communities and thus places investment and economic development at the core of community development (Taub 2004). In marked contrast to the nonprofit service-oriented approach of the CDC model, the CDFI model posits that the profit motive can be fruitfully harnessed to community development (Curtis 2006; Taub 2004). Regarding resident participation, CDFIs are under no mandate to seat resident citizens on their boards. Indeed, under the CDFI schema, a resident who merely opens a bank account is considered a participant (Taub 2004). As a theoretical model, the approach represents the nadir of resident participation in community development.

Professionalization: Too Much or Too Little?

Despite the shift to professionalization, or perhaps because of it, community development initiatives have generally failed to achieve the overarching goal of transforming distressed places into vibrant communities. Two streams of thought offer conflicting explanations as to why this is the case. One argues that professionalization has gone too far, delinking community development from residents and fostering the capture of initiatives by local elites and CDIS organizations (Dasgupta and Beard 2007; Hickey and Mohan 2005; Shortall 2004; Shucksmith 2000). In this view, terms like *resident-driven* function to legitimize programs whose benefits systematically accrue to select groups or factions. The other viewpoint claims that professionalization has not gone far enough. It suggests that the ideals of citizen control (see Stoecker 1997) and empowerment (Boyle and Silver 2005) have become ideological obstacles to the development of more professionalized approaches with greater resources while contributing to the proliferation of small, largely ineffective initiatives that have too few resources (Schafft and Greenwood 2003; Shortall 2004; Stoecker 1997).

Not surprisingly, calls for a new synthetic approach that recognizes both the importance of resident participation as well as its limits, on the one hand, and the need for greater professionalization and stronger implementing organizations as well as the dangers they present, on the other, has emerged from this debate. Fagotto and Fung (2006) and Stoecker (1997), among others, argue that strong organizations—defined as having access to significant financial resources, staffed by skilled community development professionals, and capable of forming bridging relationships between various institutional sectors—are needed to lead the work of implementation. Stoecker (1997) offers a high-capacity multilocal (for example, citywide or regional) CDC as an example of what such an organization might look like. Proponents of this approach emphasize, however, that placing strong organizations at the center of implementation presents problems of accountability that need to be countered by broad and multifaceted opportunities for resident participation (see Fagotto and Fung 2006:651–652; Stoecker 1997).

Assessing the Work on the Ground: A Multimethod Approach

This paper emerged from our evaluation of the efforts of two organizations to implement community and economic development in the

Mississippi Delta. The project began in 2003 when a national philanthropy invited a regional foundation and a CDFI to develop and implement resident-driven models of community and economic development in the Delta. The organizations took two very different approaches. The foundation developed a citizen mobilization approach grounded in the ethic of citizen control. In contrast, the CDFI developed a bank-centered model that incorporated citizen input but was driven by a professional staff of community development bankers. Significant differences in organizational structure and approach to resident participation provided an opportunity for comparative study of how the type of professional implementing organization affects resident participation and initiative outcomes.

Primary data were collected through multiple methods during two-and-a-half years of fieldwork (February 2005–July 2007). Two rounds of in-depth interviews were conducted with key informants, some of whom were involved in the initiatives and some of whom were not. These included directors and staff of local CDCs, community colleges, health agencies, schools, economic-development agencies, and chambers of commerce. We also interviewed political officials, including mayors, county judges, and supervisors. Many hours were spent observing the meetings of the resident councils established by each initiative, and focus groups were conducted with these groups during the summer of 2007. We met regularly with the staff of the implementing organizations and conducted formal interviews with those individuals in charge of directing the implementation process. Finally, all major program documents and plans were reviewed.

These data allow us to analyze the microprocesses and politics (McAreavey 2006) of community development in the understudied and particularly inauspicious context of the Mississippi Delta. In so doing, we answer the call in the literature for more empirical examinations of the relationship between professionalization and resident participation in community development (Schafft and Greenwood 2003). Although our findings are limited in terms of their ability to be generalized—few places in the United States reflect the social-institutional conditions found in the Delta—they provide insights and raise fundamental questions of interest to community development scholars.

Doing Community Development in the Delta: Race and Institutional Context

Green and Haines (2002) note that economic and political conditions in the United States at the beginning of the twenty-first century are not promising for community development work. Decades of economic restructuring marked by deindustrialization and retrenchment of federal government support for distressed places have heightened the barriers to community development (Taub 2004). In this neoliberal context, it is imperative that community development initiatives build new relationships of cooperation between the historically separate worlds of the community sector, on the one hand, and the business sector on the other (Flora, Flora, and Fey 2004; Fluharty 2004; Logan and Molotch 1987; Sharp, Flora, and Killacky 2003).

Building such bridges will, of course, be difficult. Even under the best economic, civic, and political conditions, community development initiatives that have sought to do so have encountered significant obstacles and achieved limited success (Giloth and Dewitt 1995). The barriers are far higher in places like the Delta where the racial divide and its institutional legacies present what are arguably the most inauspicious conditions in the nation for community development. There is no denying that race remains a major obstacle to progress in the Delta. For example, poverty rates among blacks in the three counties examined here are roughly five times greater than those among whites (approximately 50 percent versus 10 percent) (U.S. Census Bureau 2000). Moreover, residential segregation by race is marked, with the poor concentrated in black ghettos located across the tracks from affluent white neighborhoods and in tiny, isolated rural hamlets. The racial divide is further reinforced by the near-total segregation of schools (Duncan 1999). Finally, civil society is also fractured by race as churches, political parties, fraternal organizations and, as our findings show, community development initiatives tend to be either black or white (see Duncan 1999; Lehmann 1991).

These conditions undermine efforts at comprehensive and inclusive community development. The concentration of poverty within African-American communities that are spatially and socially isolated from more affluent white communities, combined with the fact that most white Delta residents have never acknowledged the full effects of racism (Moye 2004), has led to the adoption of a view of the poor as an underclass: they are seen as members of a deviant subculture lacking a work ethic and sustained by a permissive welfare state (Duncan 1999). This perspective has long functioned to justify the white community's neglect of the myriad problems that afflict the region and whose negative impacts are felt primarily within the black community. This neglect, in turn, has contributed to the hardening of the lack of trust felt by many African-American leaders, especially the older generation, toward white leaders (Lehmann 1991; Moye 2004).

Not surprisingly, then, participation in community development is structured by race. Indeed, community development initiatives in the Delta are inherently connected to the Civil Rights Movement and its institutionalization. They tend to be seen, as one white respondent put it, as "black initiatives" serving the black community and the black middle class, which usually dominates the leadership of organizations within the Delta's CDIS. In studying the Delta, it must be remembered that it was but forty years ago that the Voting Rights Act, along with other Great Society legislation, ended official segregation and allowed African Americans—for the first time since Reconstruction—to assume positions of power in the political and administrative spheres (Lehmann 1991; Perry 1980; Quadagno 1994). Insofar as this coincided with the rise of the professional service community development model and significant federal funding for distressed rural areas, black leaders became key actors in the emergent Delta CDIS (Duncan 1999; Lehmann 1991; Quadagno 1994). As political officials of all racial and ethnic backgrounds in the United States are prone to do, many leaders distributed the jobs, contracts, and opportunities made available through community development on the basis of self-interest and political patronage (Cobb 1992; Duncan 1999; Lehmann 1991; see also Marwell 2004 for an urban case).

One legacy of the history is that participants in community development initiatives tend to be almost exclusively black. This is because (1) the problems addressed by community development are concentrated within the black community; (2) black professionals are concentrated in the nonprofit and government sectors; and (3) the white-dominated business sector does not involve itself, because the perception of its members is that such initiatives are welfare programs for the black middle class. Silverman (2004) documented the racialized separation of the community and business spheres in Jackson, Mississippi where an African-American-dominated community development sector and a largely white business sector functioned as closed networks. Agnitsch, Flora, and Ryan (2006) found a similar structural exclusiveness along the color line in a study of the Delta (see also Brown et al. 2002; Sharp, Flora, and Killacky 2003).

Grassroots Versus Professionalized Approaches to Resident-Driven Development in the Delta

Established in the early 1990s, the foundation examined here was based in a Southeastern metropolitan city and had more than a decade of experience administering grants from a variety of national philanthropies throughout the region. It had a staff of approximately twelve full-time individuals, all of whom resided outside the Delta and far from the two target counties. Because the foundation lacked a sizable endowment, significant portions of its grant funds were dedicated to operational costs.

The foundation assigned two professional staff and one administrative assistant—all of whom were African-American women—to direct the ambitious initiative examined here. Neither of the professionals had any experience implementing a community development initiative. They sought to overcome these limitations by entering into multiple contracts with nationally and regionally based consultants, partnering with select local community-based organizations, and relying heavily on the labor of resident participants. Because the staff was not embedded in their target counties, the breadth and depth of their network connections to local residents and leadership groups were relatively thin.

In its approach to community development, the foundation staff emphasized the pursuit of equity through the empowerment of the socially excluded. They saw the persistence of poverty and extreme inequality in the Delta fundamentally as a problem of leadership: "[T]he private sector and select community leaders . . . [are] not ensuring that low-wealth people receive the benefits of programs" (Foundation Proposal 2003). They therefore argued that improving quality of life for all residents of the Delta required a resident-driven approach built around developing the capacity of the grass roots to play a leadership role and hold traditional leaders accountable. In terms of community development theory, their approach reflected the ideal of citizen control (see Arnstein 1969) whereby the intended beneficiaries of an initiative assume full responsibility for planning and implementation. Thus, early implementation activities focused almost exclusively on garnering the input and participation of residents of high-poverty neighborhoods through conducting door-to-door surveys of needs and funding a grassroots leadership-training seminar. They also organized community discussions on race and reconciliation. By surveying and training the grass roots, as well as facilitating interracial dialogue, the foundation pursued its ultimate goal of uniting new leaders with traditional leaders on resident councils that would steer the initiative.

In terms of process, the foundation's approach was strongly democratic. Seats on the council were distributed across the counties in proportion to population to ensure that residents of the small hamlets had a voice. They also mandated that council members be democratically elected by their peers. Finally, their proposal mandated that at least 51 percent of the council seats be held by nontraditional (for example, grassroots) leaders.

In practice, the foundation's focus on the grass roots was experienced as exclusion by the community sector's traditional leaders (directors of nonprofits and the like), igniting feelings of resentment among them. Thus, when those leaders were eventually recruited to join the process (about one year later), many declined. Not surprisingly, members of the business community were also conspicuously absent from the process in both counties. Finally, the councils were disproportionately staffed by black residents. In one county in which the population was roughly 50 percent white, whites comprised less than 10 percent of active council members. In sum, the resident councils were largely composed of blacks who were either newly trained grassroots leaders or representatives of grant-seeking organizations of the CDIS, including employees and directors of CDCs and government agencies. Although enthusiastic, the grassroots members generally lacked the skills and experience needed to direct a comprehensive community development initiative. This left the representatives of the CDIS organizations effectively in control.

Although the foundation was focused on mobilizing grassroots residents during the first year of implementation, it failed to invest any funds in either county on tangible projects. This lack of "hard" impacts concerned participants who were anxious to see evidence that their time and efforts would not go to waste. It was also of concern to the national funder, which was becoming concerned with the pace of the project and beginning to pressure the foundation—as one staff member put it—to "get some monies into the communities." This led the staff to approach nonprofits, schools, and other institutions to solicit proposals for small grants. According to leaders who were solicited to write grants, including one who reportedly "dropped everything" to do so, the staff promised them that their proposals would be funded. At the same time, they contracted with an external consultant to work with the two resident councils to draft five-year, countywide, comprehensive strategic plans that were rushed to completion over the course of only six weeks. Although the plans drew heavily on the data collected through the needs assessments, they contained almost no input from the business sector or the traditional leaders. The result was a set of documents that were not so much strategic plans as wish lists of disconnected projects and services desired by the residents surveyed. The national funder rejected the plans and all of the proposals submitted with them because of their lack of integration and coherence.

It is important to note here that foundation staff did recognize the urgency of making timely and tangible impacts. They did not, however, possess the organizational resources with which to do so in the event that the national funder rejected their proposals. When this occurred, it dealt a blow to the foundation's credibility among resident participants and local leaders—from which it never recovered.

Despite the rejection of their strategic plans, the resident councils proceeded with the work of implementation. Participants were largely responsible for doing the labor-intensive work of researching opportunities, drafting proposals, and developing partnerships with other entities. Despite the assistance of yet another team of external consultants, the generally poor quality of the proposals and the time it took to produce them indicated, not surprisingly, a lack of capacity among resident participants to implement comprehensive community development more or less on their own.

We began observing resident council meetings shortly after the councils were formed (about eighteen months into the initiative). During the first few meetings we observed, approximately twenty-two of the thirty-five elected members in each county were in attendance. At that point, no funding had been allocated for any tangible project. A notable aspect of these meetings was the amount of time the foundation staff and their consultants spent trying to assuage resident complaints. As months passed and funds failed to materialize, participants become visibly frustrated and many began to drop out, so that by the two-year mark the number of active participants in each county had fallen to about twelve individuals. Importantly, a large percentage of them were associated with grant-seeking organizations. Indeed, in one of the counties a single organization authored its two main grant proposals, one of which was reported to be an unfunded proposal from a previous initiative that was simply pulled off the shelf. Rather than subjecting these proposals to serious scrutiny, resident participants—clearly demoralized after completing two years of work to no apparent effect—blithely approved them, seemingly in the hope that something tangible might result from their efforts.

Interviews with key informants indicate that the foundation failed to construct a participatory structure that was representative, functional, or legitimate in the eyes of participants or the wider community. The major factors contributing to this outcome were the lack of visible impacts and the initial exclusion of the traditional leadership. The effect of the lack of impacts on participation was predictable; residents will not spend their time attending meetings and working on projects once they appear to be futile. The effect of the initial lack of attention on local leaders, however, was not as clearly predictable and points to the extreme degree of "turfism" within the Delta's CDIS. As one traditional leader explained, being "excluded" led him and others to see the initiative as a threat, an attempt to set up an alternative authority structure.

Another traditional leader pointed out that all of the funding dispersed to his county had been channeled through one particular CDC.

In the highly politicized context of the Delta CDIS, this raised questions about the integrity of the foundation staff and their process: "Everything seems to run through [the same CDC]. The two are synonymous. You might want it to be more autonomous." Although foundation leaders argued, perhaps correctly, that the select CDC was the only organization in the county with any capacity, their exclusive funding practices created resentment among other organizational leaders and bolstered the ever-present suspicion that they were more concerned with supporting their favored agency than with promoting broad development across the county.

Grassroots resident participants were also highly critical of the process and expressed their frustration largely by exiting. Their primary reason for leaving was loss of faith that the foundation could deliver on its promises of funding. Their experience was captured in the words of one who stated, "[T]hey haven't delivered on anything. . . . We'd be willing to participate *if we were confident that it would amount to something*. . . . As it is, it merely adds to the list of meetings we need to go to. It's been a waste of time and money" (emphasis added). They had also grown tired of the foundation staff's poor management of basic logistics which, for example, resulted in meetings that usually started late, ran late, were often canceled and rescheduled at the last minute, and rarely completed their agendas. Even the most sympathetic respondents—for example, an employee of the favored CDC—characterized their attempt to implement "grassroots-led" community and economic development in the Delta as "naïve," stating, "The grass roots should have a voice, but with this initiative that was all that was there. They need people who can affect change."

Finally, the initiative made no progress whatsoever in bridging the nonprofit sector with the business and banking sectors. Indeed, it merely reinforced these leaders' negative stereotype of community development. One white business-sector leader, who declined an invitation to participate, captured his faction's view as follows:

> We've been through so many of these initiatives here. It's not a new concept at all. . . . Dollars supposedly come to the area, they go to hire people and [hold] conferences. They're not effective. . . . Seems to always be the same group; *they support themselves, not the community*. . . . It's . . . a welfare mentality.

You need bankers and money folks . . . but [we] will not get involved due to the welfare mentality" (emphasis added).

More than anything else, the foundation's inability to make timely and visible impacts undermined its efforts. After years of meetings and planning sessions, the foundation and resident participants could point to only a handful of grants made as a result of their work. And while the grant-funded projects met important needs—including an affordable housing development, a youth baseball league, and an after-school activities program—their scope was limited and visible only to those who directly benefited from them. They did not contribute to the development of new network relationships and thus were of little significance to the development of broader community fields (Wilkinson 1988). Although they initially succeeded at recruiting and training a cadre of grassroots participants, their inability to leverage their efforts into impacts led to exit. Additionally, the traditional leaders who initially resented being excluded from the initiative declined later invitations. During our interviews, some derided as "pathetic" and "a joke the initiative's leadership—the foundation staff, grassroots participants, and the external consultants—for their inability to deliver funding projects. Instead of establishing councils in which new grassroots leaders worked in concert with more traditional leaders for the benefit of the entire county, the interaction of the foundation's process with local conditions allowed local CDIS organizations essentially to capture the initiatives. After two-and-a-half years of work, the foundation suspended its initiative indefinitely in both counties.

The CDFI and Its Professionally Managed Model

The second initiative we evaluated was implemented by a CDFI. The CDFI's target community was one county; however, in practice it focused its activities almost exclusively on the urban center (population roughly 15,000) in which its office and parent bank were physically located. The CDFI began its community lending operations in the area circa 2000. By community development standards, as an implementing organization it exhibited a very high degree of professionalization. The staff consisted of a diverse group of five locally based and full-time community development professionals that included men and women, blacks and whites, and locals and outsiders who had moved to the area specifically to work on the project. Importantly, the CDFI's association with a bank gave it access to an enormous amount of financial capital by community development standards and afforded it a large degree of independence from the national funder. The bank association, combined with the locally based staff, provided a degree of connection to and influence within the business community rarely seen in community development.

The CDFI's analysis of past Delta initiatives concluded that they had failed to benefit the majority of residents because they lacked leadership, emphasized services over economic growth, and were largely oriented towards serving the particularistic interests of CDIS organizations. The CDFI also recognized that the lack of meaningful impacts had left residents cynical about the value of participating in community development programs. Thus, their proposal stated: "[T]he time for additional studies, discussions, and theoretical processes is over. It is now time to do something" (CDFI Proposal 2003:5). This focus on action signaled an approach to participation that deemphasized citizen control in exchange for strategic effectiveness. Citing the "unfortunate reality" that "in many rural communities, local organizations do not have a history of cooperation due primarily to racial division and a lack of progressive community leadership," and a "near total lack of capacity" in their target county, they proposed using their organization—its "comprehensive and integrated network of for-profit and nonprofit entities"—to serve as an "initial 'freestanding' planning system" and "bridge organization between [sic] local community development organizations" (CDFI Proposal 2003:5).

Although the typical CDFI approach sees lack of access to capital as the major problem in high-poverty locales (Taub 2004), the one examined here also recognized that new institutional relationships were required to create the conditions necessary to attract investment to a declining community and leverage it into community-wide outcomes. This entailed partnering with middle-class and elite residents who were pursuing a root-and-branch reconstruction of the institutional infrastructure of the county, including local government, economic development agencies, the school systems, the health-care system, and beyond.

The CDFI rejected the view that community development initiatives fail because of too much professionalization and the exclusion of the grass roots. Rather, in their view the problem stems from the related issues of a lack of professionalization and the nonparticipation of the middle-class and business sectors, which together facilitated capture by the CDIS. Recruiting these groups required the CDFI to demonstrate that their initiative would differ from past efforts in at least two crucial respects: One, it would affect immediate and visible impacts, and two, it would not allow capture, or even the perception of it, by CDIS organizations.[1] It was with this goal in mind that the CDFI proposal posited itself as a freestanding planning system within the community.

In theory, their model of resident participation was bifurcated into two discrete phases—a year-long strategic planning phase followed by the implementation of projects. The planning phase consisted of a series of surveys and open meetings run by a facilitator with expertise in conflict resolution. The purpose was to garner input from all sectors of the community to be used in the development of a five-year countywide comprehensive strategic plan. Over three hundred residents, including leaders of CDCs serving low-wealth residents, were documented as participating. It is important to note that, in reality, the planning was accompanied by a number of strategic investments made by the staff, who used bank funds to restore historic buildings and reduce dilapidated housing, among other things. Because these investments were concentrated in the downtown district of the county seat and well advertised as part of the initiative, they presented clear signs of change that residents associated with the initiative.

In contrast to the openness of the planning phase, the role of residents in implementation was very limited and highly selective. To facilitate achievement of impacts, the CDFI staff, in their own words, "hand-picked" a small group of residents to participate in implementation on the basis of their "integrity and capacity." To combat patronage, or the impression of it, they structured resident participation along three "branches" to form a system of "checks and balances." One branch consisted of target-area subcommittees (for example, health, education, and leadership) to work with CDFI staff on developing grant proposals. The committees were chaired by residents with expertise in each area. Another branch consisted of a twelve-member oversight board. Their role was highly limited and consisted of approving or rejecting only those proposals that did not clearly fit within the purview of the community-approved five-year strategic plan. Finally, the third branch consisted of a small group of elites with expertise in finance, business, and law. Their role was to evaluate the importance, feasibility, and integrity of every proposal before it was submitted to the national funder. While the selection of participants by CDFI staff violated a basic tenet of community development theory and impugned, to some extent, the claim that the initiative was resident driven, interviews with participants and observers indicate that it did send the desired signal to the middle class, that is, that theirs was a serious initiative intended to make major changes in the community and thus did not represent community development as usual in the Delta.

Nonetheless, the selected participants were racially diverse, largely men, and drawn exclusively from the middle and upper classes. A significant percentage had recently moved to the area or returned to it after having spent years living and working elsewhere (for instance, Chicago and Los Angeles). Their backgrounds covered a range of institutional sectors and included running businesses, schools, and medical institutions, among other things. Rather than relying on these individuals to do the heavy lifting of implementation, the staff did the work of researching opportunities, developing partnerships, writing grants, and coordinating activities. In terms of logistics, the staff ensured that meeting notifications were sent out well in advance, meetings were tightly run, and projects proceeded in a timely fashion. Thus, resident participants functioned, as one staff put it, "more like a board of directors of a corporation"—that is, they attended monthly meetings during which they were apprised of staff activities, provided input, and offered their knowledge and network connections to facilitate the work.

Data collected through interviews with residents both involved and not involved in the initiative, as well as with a focus group held with ten members of the oversight board, indicated that the initiative was indeed experienced and perceived as different. Participants were unanimous in the view that they could see the effects of their work and believed that their participation, while limited, was contributing to a groundwork upon which long-term community transformation could be built. Their sense of effectiveness and hope was highly related to the many financial investments made by the CDFI and its parent bank during the planning and early implementation phase.[2] The credibility these investments lent to the initiative was captured in the words of one participant who stated, "Where others gave a lot of lip service, [they] delivered product."

Despite some reservations regarding the CDFI's tight management of the initiative, resident perceptions of its leadership were overwhelmingly positive. The staff was characterized as "a tremendous resource." One local businessman reflected the general view of those interviewed who were in that sector when he opined, "They understand people like me," meaning, they "get things done." Additionally, the staff, all of whom lived in the area, were seen as sincerely interested in the development of the community as opposed to merely furthering organizational interests. For example, some respondents noted individual staff participation in community-oriented activities sponsored by other local groups. In the context of the Delta this was seen as unusual.

In addition to contributing to the achievement of "hard" short-term impacts (we use the term *contributing to* to indicate that in some cases the CDFI played more of a complimentary than lead role), respondents credited the initiative with facilitating the emergence of "new hope" and a "can-do spirit." Noting the continuing relevance of the racial divide, participants characterized it as a rallying point and a vehicle that individuals who would not normally sit down together could "plug into" to discuss common concerns.

Resident criticisms of the CDFI were limited but significant. Not surprisingly, some characterized it as a case of professionalization gone too far. For example, more than one member of the oversight board stated that he or she had no real role to play and functioned as little more than a rubber stamp for projects developed by the staff. A concern was also expressed that the CDFI might become too powerful within the community and that in the future perhaps all proposed

economic and community development efforts—"by any group"—
would have to "be funneled through them." Perhaps the most frequently voiced concern, however, was that the CDFI had not done
enough to reach out to the low-wealth community in the process. A
number of elite resident participants noted that if the initiative were to
achieve its goal of improving quality of life "for all residents of the
county, not merely those ready and able to take advantage of the opportunities," much stronger efforts to engage low-wealth residents were
needed.

Discussion and Conclusions

The initiatives examined here present cases of (1) a less- versus more-
professionalized approach to community development implemented
by (2) a relatively weak versus strong organization. In this section, we
discuss how the variation in short-term outcomes achieved by these
different types of approaches and organizations speak to community
development theory and what they recommend for future initiatives in
high-poverty, racially divided rural areas.

The foundation's grassroots-led effort followed a parallel path to
failure in both of its target counties. Why? Was failure due to its application of a strong version of the citizen-control approach that led it
to overlook the lack of local resources, particularly in the area of leadership, and the deep-seated conflicts in both of its target counties? Or,
was it due to the fact that as an implementing organization it lacked
the resources necessary to carry through its model successfully? Our
case studies do not allow us to consider these hypotheses independently. It seems plausible, however, that the foundation chose a citizen-
control approach, at least in part, because it was a weak organization.
As a weak organization the foundation had little choice but to pursue
an approach that relied heavily on local assets in the form of
community-based organizations, regional consultants, and community
residents. This proved infeasible, however, in the highly competitive
and politicized CDIS of the Delta, where its focus on the grass roots
made enemies of traditional leaders and its targeting of funds to a limited number of local organizations triggered immediate allegations of
favoritism-and-community development-as-usual. Importantly, its inability to make investments independently of the national funder left it

with no capacity to make the types of timely and strategic investments that helped earn the CDFI credibility.

It is important to recognize that the foundation found intellectual justification for its approach in a partial or selective reading of the community development literature that took from it a strong version of the citizen-control thesis while overlooking the importance of organizations. Their reading of the literature likely combined with organizational interests to produce a number of missteps. By focusing tightly on the ideal of resident empowerment so strongly emphasized in the literature, they overestimated the capacities of grassroots participants, underestimated both the importance and the difficulties associated with bridging the community and business sectors, and overlooked the anticommunity-building dynamics inherent in the CDIS. Moreover, their use of the rhetoric of citizen control in their proposal allowed them to garner monies from the national funder to support operations in not one, but two large counties.[3] This had the effect of increasing the amount of operations funding for the foundation—a positive outcome from the organization's point of view—while at the same time reducing the likelihood that the initiative would succeed in either target county. Following the collapse of their initiative, one of the professional staff stated that their approach had been "naïve." The data indicate that one cost of their learning experience was to exacerbate the cynicism of local residents toward externally initiated community development initiatives.

That said, it is important to recognize that the foundation's approach did produce some positive results which, had the foundation had more resources, could have contributed to wider development. The leadership trainings, discussions on racial reconciliation, and resident leadership councils did have meaningful impact for some at the individual level. For example, one white leader who participated in a discussion on race reported being deeply moved and enlightened by an African-American woman's account of her experience of racism. In another case, a grassroots leader who received leadership training went before her county board of supervisors to advocate for a water system for her rural hamlet. Additionally, there were also important hard outputs, such as a youth baseball league, which addressed pressing needs that would otherwise have gone unmet. Ultimately, however, these effects were not felt beyond program participants, were scattered across a wide expanse of geographic space, and thus failed to provide a foundation on which broader and sustainable community development could be pursued (see Schafft and Greenwood 2003).

Similarly, the CDFI could not have taken its approach were it not a strong organization. In contrast the CDFI saw the citizen-control model as fundamentally implausible in the Delta given its CDIS, the limits of grassroots participants, and the chasm between leaders in the business sector and those in the area of community development—including local government. They understood the extent to which the long-term viability of the county depended on broad institutional restructuring (for example, making improvements in basic infrastructure, upgrading the quality of education and political leadership, and creating linkages to regional economic actors) and thus made strategic decisions to (1) work with residents with higher capacities in terms of financial and human capital and (2) allow their professional staff the flexibility to implement a strategic plan built on input from the community without having to include the community in a deliberative processes over every step (see Sojourner et al. 2004 for a similar approach). In explaining the CDFI's success at garnering and retaining middle-class participants, the roles of its professional staff and financial resources cannot be overstated (see Austin 2000). These resources made possible the investments and tangible outcomes that piqued the interest of residents, muted criticism from naysayers, and allowed the CDFI to operate largely independently of both the local CDIS and the national funder. In sum, the CDFI's status as a strong organization allowed it to achieve its goals of immediate impacts and credibility with the middle class. These achievements, in turn, facilitated nascent relationships of cooperation between local leaders long factionalized by the racialized institutionalization of group interests.

The CDFI's approach was not without problems of significant concern to community development scholars and practitioners. Its view that the target community lacked local assets, especially in the area of leadership, led to the underutilization of residents in implementation. Its elite approach to participation in a county in which poverty is widespread raises the question of whether the initiative truly represents resident-driven community development or the construction of a rural "growth machine" (Flora, Flora, and Fey 2004; Logan and Molotch 1987). These concerns must be considered, however, in light of the high barriers faced by the CDFI—its resources notwithstanding—which, as witnessed in the demise of the foundation's efforts, indicate a need for some degree of elite participation and centralized control. It must also be noted that, as more than a few respondents stated, the CDFI did initially outreach to leaders of grassroots organizations; however, those organizations had subsequently quit. As one put it, "You can invite people to participate but that does not mean they will. There are some who, if they cannot control it, will not participate."

The observed differences in short-term outcomes, participant experiences, and resident perceptions of the initiatives speak to questions of interest to community development theory. Regarding the question of the relationship between professionalization and resident participation, the ideal of citizen control established in Arnstein's (1969) "ladder model" posits an inverse relationship between professionalization and resident participation such that greater professionalization necessarily detracts from resident control (Schafft and Greenwood 2003). The empirical literature indicates, however, that resident participation is strongly correlated with timely achievement of visible impacts (Green and Haines 2002; Kubisch et al. 2002) and that the production of such impacts is related to professionalization (Fagotto and Fung 2006). The proliferation of initiatives that eschew professionalization in the name of citizen control, despite numerous studies indicating the limits of their impacts, indicates that Arstein's ideal today is not only more often than not a "myth" (Stoecker 1997) but—and perhaps this is more problematic— has become an ideology.

Our findings not only support the argument for greater professionalization but also suggest that some types of organizations are better suited to leading such initiatives than others, especially in conflict-ridden local contexts like the Delta. The CDFI's resource base allowed it to pursue an action-oriented approach that challenged the normal operation of the CDIS. This, in turn, facilitated the engagement of the business sector and, ultimately, led to limited yet significant instances of interracial and intersectoral collaboration. Conversely, the foundation's lack of resources left it dependent on local residents and CDIS organizations; this set hard limits on what could be achieved long before the first meetings with community residents were held.

Another problem with the strong version of the citizen-control approach highlighted by our findings is that—to the extent that it allows for professional organizations at all—they should function as relatively distant facilitators of communication among local groups rather than active participants. Leeuwis (2000) cites this view as flawed for assuming that factions in distressed areas actually do share underlying sets of common interests and that "undistorted" communication will lead to enlightenment and cooperation. He notes how community development initiatives typically begin with efforts to bring everyone in the community together to agree on a vision and a set of steps to achieve it. He characterizes this as naïve insofar as the problems that plague distressed communities are rooted in real conflicts and that it is often in the rational interest of some factions to oppose projects—especially those they cannot control. He develops a model of resident participation and professionalization that conceptualizes the organization not as a facilitator but as an actively engaged "negotiator" of conflict among groups (2000:942; see also Sojourner et al. 2004). In this role, the implementing organization must have the capacity to act strategically to create conditions through which factionalized groups may—over the long-term—come together to engage in deliberation over a common vision. He describes such an organization as follows:

> [An organization] needs to have an active strategy, resources, and a power-base in order to forge sustainable agreements. For example, [they] may, at a certain point, have to strategically select participants and exclude others, put pressure on certain stakeholders and/or impose sanctions if actors do not follow the agreed rules of conduct, etc. In order to achieve this, the [negotiator] needs—in addition to the power-base provided by the agreed rules of conduct—a certain amount of status, credibility, charisma, influence, and trustworthiness (Leeuwis 2000:950).

From this perspective, bringing all relevant stakeholders together to create a vision for a community change makes sense only during the latter stages of an initiative (Leeuwis 2000:950). To a large extent, the strategic-selective approach of the CDFI to resident participation reflects Leeuwis's model.

Although our findings indicate support for such an approach in the Delta, they also warrant issuing a number of serious cautions. Most significantly, to date the CDFI's approach to the low-income community has been unarguably paternalistic. No low-income residents were selected to serve in positions of leadership because, as one staff explained, "low-income people are concerned with how they are going to pay the rent or obtain their next meal. They don't have the time or interest, or, to be frank, skills needed to participate in planning meetings that will not show results for five or ten years. That's a luxury you and I share." There is also concern that the benefits of projects initiated in the name of the "community" will accrue mainly to business-sector elites while burdening other elements of the community. For example, a CDFI-led beautification project included the abatement of a slum in which approximately twenty families resided. While the condition of the housing was by all accounts abhorrent, efforts to ensure that displaced residents obtained adequate and affordable alternative housing were weak—they were provided moving expenses and one month's rent at their new abode—and no follow-up analysis of the effects of the move on their well-being was conducted.

At the same time, the CDFI's paternalism also reflects the fact that the resources of time, money, and, importantly, patience on the part of community members are limited and thus mandate that choices be made and trade-offs accepted. Reflecting Leeuwis' approach, the staff assessed the importance of low-wealth resident participation in relation to the achievement of other strategic goals and concluded that it would be a goal to be achieved incrementally over time. As one staff stated, "Once you have a system up and running that people can plug into—once you can show a record of success and demonstrate to folks they won't be wasting their time—that's when it makes sense to bring in the low-income."

In our view, the ideals of citizen control and resident empowerment are indispensable as both the means and ends of community development. However, this study indicates that, to the extent that they can function as ideological obstacles to professionalization and strong organizations, privileging them as means may undercut their achievement, over the long-term, as ends. The foundation asked far too much of its resident participants while delivering far too little in supports, resources, and, ultimately, impacts. Thus, they replicated the well-documented path of lack of impacts, participant exit, capture by CDIS organizations, and termination. Beyond garnering input on goals, the CDFI's professional approach asked little of resident participants while delivering much in the way of immediate and visible impacts. These impacts imparted a sense of effectiveness and "hope" among participants, won the respect of the middle-class and business sectors, and attracted the attention of local residents as well as regional leaders. To a far greater extent than the foundation's, the CDFI's initiative contributed to the beginnings of new, pragmatically oriented communication and cooperation across historically divided leadership factions, thereby laying a tentative foundation for resident-led comprehensive community development over the long term.

Notes

1. Of course, the CDFI itself and its associated nonprofit organizations are also part of the broader CDIS. The foundation, the national funder, and we as evaluators are also participants in the industry.

2. In addition to the restoration of the historic buildings and abatement of dilapidated housing, other notable investments were made in the areas of K–12 education, after-school activities, affordable housing, and health care.

3. The foundation initially sought funding to implement their initiative in three counties, but this was rejected by the national funder.

References

Agnitsch, Kerry, Jan Flora, and Vern Ryan. 2006. "Bonding and bridging social capital: The interactive effects on community development." *Journal of the Community Development Society* 37:36–51.

Aigner, Stephen M., Cornelia B. Flora, and Juan M. Hernandez. 2001. "The premise and promise of citizenship and civil society for renewing democracies and empowering sustainable communities." *Sociological Inquiry* 71:493–507.

Arnstein, Sherry R. 1969. "A ladder of citizen participation." *Journal of the American Planning Association* 35:216–224.

Austin, James E. 2000. "Business leadership coalitions." *Business and Society Review* 105:305–322.

Boyle, Mary Ellen, and Ira Silver. 2005. "Poverty, partnerships and privilege: Elite institutions and community empowerment." *City and Community* 4:233–53.

Brown, Prudence, and Leila Fiester. 2007. *Hard Lessons About Philanthropy and Community Change from the Neighborhood Improvement Initiative.* Chicago, IL: Chapin Hall.

Brown, Ralph, Albert B. Nylander III, Brayden G. King, and Benjamin J. Lough. 2002. "Growth machine attitudes and community development in two racially diverse rural Mississippi Delta communities: A monolithic approach in a complex region." *Journal of the Community Development Society* 31:173–195.

CDFI Proposal. 2003.

Clark, David, Rebekah Southern, and Julian Beer. 2007. "Rural governance, community empowerment, and the new institutionalism: A case study of the Isle of Wight." *Journal of Rural Studies* 23:254–266.

Cobb, James C. 1992. *The Most Southern Place on Earth: The Mississippi Delta and the Roots of Regional Identity.* New York: Oxford University Press.

Curtis, Brandy. 2006. "An overview of the CDFI industry." Pp. 1–7 in *New England Community Developments.* Boston, MA: Federal Reserve Bank of Boston.

Dasgupta, Aniruddha, and Victoria A. Beard. 2007. "Community driven development, collective action and elite capture in Indonesia." *Development and Change* 38:229–249.

Duncan, Cynthia M. 1999. *Worlds Apart: Why Poverty Persists in Rural America.* New Haven, CT: Yale University Press.

Fagotto, Elena, and Archon Fung. 2006. "Empowered participation in urban governance: The Minneapolis Neighborhood Revitalization Program." *International Journal of Urban and Regional Research* 30:638–55.

Flora, Cornelia B., Jan L. Flora, and Susan Fey. 2004. *Rural Communities: Legacy and Change.* Boulder, CO: Westview Press.

Fluharty, Charles W. 2004. "Assessing the state of rural governance in the United States." Center for the Study of Rural America, Federal Reserve Bank of Kansas City. www.kansascityfed.org/PUBLICAT/NewGovernance04/Fluharty04.pdf

Foundation Proposal. 2003.

Frisch, Michael, and Lisa J. Servon. 2006. "CDCs and the changing context of urban community development: A review of the field and the environment." *Journal of the Community Development Society* 37:88–108.

Giloth, Robert, and John Dewitt. 1995. "Mobilizing civic infrastructure: Foundation supported job generation." *National Civic Review* 84:196–210.

Gittell, Marilyn. 1980. *Limits to Citizen Participation: The Decline of Community Organizations.* Beverly Hills, CA: Sage Publications.

Green, Gary Paul, and Anna Haines. 2002. *Asset Building and Community Development*. Thousand Oaks, CA: Sage Publications.

Hardina, Donna. 2006. "Strategies for citizen participation and empowerment in non-profit, community-based organizations." *Journal of the Community Development Society* 37:4–17.

Hayward, Chris, Lyn Simpson, and Leanne Wood. 2004. "Still left out in the cold: Problematizing participatory research and development." *Sociologia Ruralis* 44:95–108.

Hickey, Sam, and Giles Mohan. 2005. "Relocating participation within a radical politics of development." *Development and Change* 36:237–262.

Krumholz, Norman, W. Dennis Keating, Philip D. Star, and Mark C. Chupp. 2006. "The long-term impact of CDCs on urban neighborhoods: Case studies of Cleveland's Broadway-Slavic Village and Tremont neighborhoods." *Journal of the Community Development Society* 37:33–52.

Kubisch, Anne C., Patricia Auspos, Prudence Brown, Robert Chaskin, Karen Fulbright-Anderson, and Ralph Hamilton. 2002. *Voices from the Field II: Reflections on Comprehensive Community Change*. Washington, DC: The Aspen Institute.

Leeuwis, Cees. 2000. "Reconceptualizing participation for sustainable rural development: Towards a negotiation approach." *Development and Change* 31:931–959.

Lehmann, Nicholas. 1991. *The Promised Land: The Great Black Migration*. New York: Alfred A. Knopf.

Logan, John R., and Harvey Molotch. 1987. *Urban Fortunes: The Political Economy of Place*. Berkeley: University of California Press.

Marwell, Nicole P. 2004. "Privatizing the welfare state: Nonprofit community organizations." *American Sociological Review* 69:265–291.

McAreavey, Ruth. 2006. "Getting close to the action: The micro-politics of rural development." *Sociologia Ruralis* 46:85–103.

Medoff, Peter, and Holly Sklar 1994. *Streets of Hope: The Fall and Rise of an Urban Neighborhood*. Boston, MA: South End Press.

Moye, J. Todd. 2004. *Let the People Decide: Black Freedom and White Resistance Movements in Sunflower County, Mississippi, 1945–1986*. Chapel Hill: University of North Carolina Press.

Orleck, Annelise. 2006. *Storming Caesar's Palace: How Black Mothers Fought Their Own War on Poverty*. Boston, MA: Beacon Press.

Parisi, Domenico, Steven M. Grice, Michael Taquino, and Duane A. Gill. 2002. "Building capacity for community efficacy for economic development in Mississippi." *Journal of the Community Development Society* 33:19–38.

Pavey, Jamey L., Allyson B. Muth, David Ostermeier, and Miriam L. E. Steiner Davis. 2007. "Building capacity for local governance: An application of interactional theory to developing a community of interest." *Rural Sociology* 72:90–110.

Perry, Huey L. 1980. "The socio-economic impact of black empowerment in a rural southern locality." *Rural Sociology* 45:207–222.

Quadagno, Jill. 1994. *The Color of Welfare: How Racism Undermined the War on Poverty.* New York: Oxford University Press.

Richards, Lynn, and Matthew Dalbey. 2006. "Creating great places: The role of citizen participation." *Journal of the Community Development Society* 37:18–32.

Schafft, Kai A., and Davydd J. Greenwood. 2003. "Promises and dilemmas of participation: Action research, search conference methodology, and community development." *Journal of the Community Development Society* 34:18–35.

Sharp, Jeff S., Jan L. Flora, and Jim Killacky. 2003. "Networks and fields: Corporate business leader involvement in voluntary organizations of a large nonmetropolitan city." *Journal of the Community Development Society* 34:36–56.

Shortall, Sandy. 2004. "Social or economic goals, civic inclusion or exclusion? An analysis of rural development theory and practice." *Sociologia Ruralis* 44:109–123.

Shucksmith, Mark. 2000. "Endogenous development, social capital, and social inclusion: Perspectives from LEADER in the UK." *Sociologia Ruralis* 40:208–219.

Silverman, Robert M. 2004. "Community development corporations (CDCs) in the deep South: The interaction of social capital, community context, and organizational networks." Pps. 125–146 in *Community-Based Organizations: The Intersection of Social Capital and Local Context in Contemporary Urban Society,* edited by Robert M. Silverman. Detroit, MI: Wayne State University Press.

Sojourner, Aaron, Prudence Brown, Robert Chaskin, Ralph Hamilton, Leila Fiester, and Harold Richman. 2004. *Moving Forward While Staying in Place: Embedded Funders and Community Change.* Chicago, IL: University of Chicago, Chapin Hall Center for Children.

Stoecker, Randy. 1997. "The CDC model of urban redevelopment: A critique and an alternative." *Journal of Urban Affairs* 19:1–22.

Taub, Richard. 2004. *Doing Development in Arkansas: Using Credit to Create Opportunity for Entrepreneurs Outside the Mainstream.* Fayetteville: University of Arkansas Press.

Tocqueville, Alexis de. 1835. *Democracy in America.* New York: Library of America, 2004.

U.S. Census Bureau. 2000. http://factfinder.census.gov.

Voth, Donald E. 1975. "An evaluation of community development programs in Illinois." *Social Forces* 53:635–647.

Wilkinson, Kenneth P. 1988. "Community crisis in the rural south." Pp. 72–86 in *The Rural South in Crisis: Challenges for the Future,* edited by Lionel J. Beaulieu. Boulder CO: Westview Press.

Wilson, William J. 1987. *The Truly Disadvantaged: The Inner City, the Underclass, and Public Policy.* Chicago, IL: University of Chicago Press.

Yin, Jordan S. 1998. "The community development industry system: A case study of politics and institutions in Cleveland, 1967–1997." *Journal of Urban Affairs* 20:137–57.

9   Lessons Learned

GARY PAUL GREEN

Asset-based community development represents a significant transformation in how community building is practiced. John Kretzmann and John McKnight conceptualized this new approach to community building in their book *Building Communities from the Inside Out: A Path Toward Finding and Mobilizing a Community's Assets* (1993). Since its publication, numerous organizations and communities have sought to build communities through the enhancement and leveraging of local resources.

In this volume, we present one of the first attempts to critically examine community asset-based development strategies. Our goal was to identify common issues and concerns, as well as build a stronger conceptual basis for community practitioners. In this chapter I review some of the key lessons learned from these case studies.

Community organizers usually develop good sense about which processes work best in different situations. Through practice, they begin to connect the processes and tactics they use with outcomes and impacts in the community. Our strategy in this project is much the same. Examining several different case studies, we seek to understand why some asset-based development efforts are more successful than others. It is challenging because we have chosen to consider asset-based development in a variety of contexts and cultures. A controlled experimental design would have examined communities in the same context, employing the same tactics. This design, however, would have limited our ability to generalize more broadly about asset-based development.

The case studies include several different types of community assets (for example, culture, natural resources, and finances) and are in a variety of contexts (for instance, central city, rural, and Native American reservations). We are interested in several different questions. What are the similarities and differences across these different assets? What are the general patterns in the process of asset-based development? What are some common challenges that communities face in asset-based development strategies? How effective are these strategies in promoting public participation? If we can identify some common linkages, it may be possible to develop a more robust understanding of asset-based development.

Case Study Themes

In each of the case studies, the authors were asked to address some common questions. What was the local context? How was the process of asset-based development initiated? What were some of the outcomes and impacts of the project? What are some of the perceived limitations and constraints to asset-based community development? Although we were interested in learning the lessons from each of the specific cases, we were also identifying commonalities and differences across the cases. There are several consistent themes in the case studies.

1. Several of the cases suggest that community assets have a multifunctional character. By multifunctional, I mean that these assets can serve a variety of functions. Natural resources are a good example because they can contribute to community well-being in a couple of different ways (Goe and Green 2005; Green 2001). Natural resources can be extracted and processed for external markets or promoted as a natural amenity to attract residents and tourists to the region (Power 1996). These different functions need not be considered in conflict with one another. It may be possible to manage these different functions in a complementary manner. For example, many communities manage their forests in a way that continues to harvest trees for processing while sustaining the forest land for its amenity value. This

complementary approach requires a conscious effort by the community to find the right balance of interests. Other communities may choose to emphasize the amenity value of the forests over the exclusion of extractive activities. This conflict is most evidence in Chapter 4 in the discussion of the conflict over a protected area in Guatemala and in Chapter 7 in the analysis of the role of natural amenities in rural development. Obviously there are interests behind how natural amenities are used. Landowners may push in one direction, while others who are interested in recreation may view the natural amenities in another way.

The implication is that communities often have more options than they think. Communities faced with vacant manufacturing facilities or warehouses may continue to try to find new tenants. Others communities may realize the potential of these sites for residential or commercial development. Asset-based development often requires communities to think differently about themselves and not necessarily get locked into viewing their resources the same way they have in the past. It also may make it more difficult to achieve consensus or some agreement on how community assets should be used.

2. A related theme is that community assets are inherently value laden. Identifying community assets is not an objective process, but instead is a social process rooted in values, culture, and interests. Community assets are not things that are identified or evaluated identically by everyone. Because assets may be interpreted in different ways, it may be useful to begin with a discussion of values as a way to frame the asset-identification process. What are some common values in the community? How are these values expressed in local organizations and institutions?

The value-laden nature of community assets is demonstrated in several of the case studies. In the study of York, Alabama (Chapter 3), the arts were identified as a critical asset in the community. Because of the segregated nature of the community, however, there was little agreement over whose culture should be featured and celebrated. In the study of Petoskey, Michigan (Chapter 7), seasonal and permanent residents held many different values and had very different preferences for the future of the community. Seasonal residents preferred managed growth that emphasized the natural amenities and the historical character of the community. Permanent residents valued economic growth and job opportunities for their families. They were less concerned with some of the community attributes that motivated seasonal residents. Although these differences were deep, the promotion of amenity-based development through tourism provided good jobs for residents while maintaining some of the key attributes of the community valued by seasonal residents.

Culture can blind us to the importance of local assets. It may be difficult for residents to recognize the importance of their assets to others. In the case study of Bellow Falls (Chapter 5), it was an outsider (an artist) who moved to the community and sparked the formation of the Rockingham Arts and Museum Project (RAMP). Thus, because local culture is often taken for granted, it may be ignored by local residents.

3. A third theme is the interdependence among community assets. Rather than isolating resources, asset-based community development relies on a holistic approach. The case studies of community development financial institutions (CDFIs) (Chapter 2) illustrates how these microcredit programs can be made more effective with education and training programs that enhance the human capital of borrowers. The Guatemalan case study (Chapter 4) demonstrates how political capital interacts with management of natural resources at the local level. Several of the cases emphasize the importance of human capital, especially leadership, in mobilizing other community assets.

Asset-based development, therefore, usually requires an understanding of the interaction of various organizations and institutions. Residents often prefer to isolate economic and social problems, focusing on a specific problem or issue. Asset-based development seeks not only to identify the key resources in communities, but also to determine how communities can build on other assets.

4. The case studies confirm that even in some of the most impoverished areas it is possible to build community capacity through mobilization of local assets. The chapter by Dewees and Sarkozy-Banoczy (Chapter 2) is probably the best example. Native American communities are among the poorest population in the United States. Yet CDFIs have been successful in helping to build wealth and financial literacy in these settings (Green and Haines 2007). The study of Chicago's west side (Chapter 6) is equally impressive. This neighborhood has high rates of poverty and unemployment, as well as numerous social prob-

lems. The community has been successful, however, at numerous projects to enhance their quality of life.

Resources are frequently overlooked by residents in impoverished communities. It is often new residents or those not in official positions of power who are able to see the potential for mobilizing these assets (Flora et al. 1992; Green et al. 1990). Women and minorities also typically provide a different view on local resources. The asset-mapping process can also play an important role in stimulating new ideas and in helping residents think beyond the problems and constraints facing the community.

This discussion does not suggest that asset-based development never taps into external resources, such as technical assistance and financial resources. Local resources are often leveraged to further build capacity. The case studies do suggest, however, that external assistance must be responsive to the local community. The case study of CDFIs on Native American reservations (Chapter 2) raises some interesting issues about local resources and sustainability. One of the key issues in microenterprise loan funds is the importance of scale to achieve sustainability. Most, if not all, of the microcredit programs must continue to rely on subsidies from foundations and other funding sources. It may be possible, however, to work across several communities to achieve sustainability.

5. Asset-based development is best implemented when communities have a clear vision of their preferred future. Decisions about mobilizing community resources need to be placed in the context of the goals of community residents. This does not necessarily mean that asset-based development is always preceded by consensus. But it can be facilitated by identifying key issues of concern across a broad base in the community. The value of community participation in identifying goals is illustrated very well in the Guatemala case.

Not all of the communities that were studied went through a formal process to identify assets. I think the evidence would suggest that it is preferable for communities to develop a vision for the future before mapping assets and developing a strategic plan (Green, Haines, and Halebsky 2000). Public participation at this stage is critical for a couple of reasons. Broad participation is necessary to identify common elements across different interests and cultures. It also provides "buy-in" to whatever plan on projects are identified.

6. The role of race and ethnicity in asset-based development is an explicit issue in several chapters. Sarah Dewees and Stewart Sarkozy-Banoczy (Chapter 2) discuss the difficulty Native Americas face in financing new businesses. Emily Blejwas (Chapter 3) points to the obstacles in mobilizing a biracial community around arts-based development in the rural South. Many of the other chapters also analyze asset-based development in minority communities. The difficulty in York (Chapter 3) is primarily that the arts movement did not adequately mobilize the African-American population, largely because of the level of racial segregation. Because the process did not adequately involve African Americans, the project was not defined in a way that would interest many minority residents.

There are excellent examples, however, of community organizing and mobilizing efforts across racial and ethnic lines, especially around educational issues (see Warren 2001). One of the difficulties in York is that the case involved not only different racial groups but also different social classes. Several of the other chapters addressed asset building within a single neighborhood that may be heterogeneous with respect to race and ethnicity but that has very little variability in social class. The important lesson here is that broad participation is necessary to successfully implement asset-based development. Depending on the issue, race, ethnicity, and social class can be difficult barriers to permeate.

What We Still Do Not Know

Communities have learned a great deal from their experience with asset-based development. Many of the traditional tools and practices used to promote development focus on external markets and attracting resources to the community. Asset-based development provides a set of tools that build on local resources.

There is still a lot to learn about asset-based development. Too many communities go through a process of mapping their assets—and nothing ever comes out of the process. Asset-based development cannot be reduced to a set of techniques or processes. It requires the broad engagement of residents to unlock community resources to benefit local people.

Several case studies raise issues that need further attention. The study in Guatemala (Chapter 4) suggests that the context for asset-based development is extremely difficult in developing countries. Dougherty and Peralta argue that the weak institutional environment in Guatemala made it difficult to hold the government accountable and to prevent corruption. In some respects, asset-based development makes some basic assumptions about the political system and the capacity for local institutions to respond to civil society. Additional work is needed to examine the effectiveness of asset-based development in international settings.

Chapter 8 raises some tough questions about the role of local-resident expertise in the asset-based development model. Harvey and Beaulieu review some of the current debates over professional expertise and local knowledge in community development processes. They tend to conclude that local control and empowerment is absolutely necessary for implementing asset-based development, but there is a need for professionalization and strong organizations as well to support these efforts. These tensions were also apparent in the case study of CDFIs for Native Americans (Chapter 2). More research is needed to explore how these different functions can best be organized. Harvey and Beaulieu suggest that large multicommunity organizations that provide technical assistance to local residents might be the best option. This does raise difficult questions about local control of assets and how professionalization that does not build dependency can be promoted. Unfortunately, we do not have many useful models for establishing these organizational models. At this point, combining community organizing and development efforts in a single organization seems to be the most appropriate model for building accountability and results into asset-based development.

There is a growing call for regional development (Dreier, Mollenkopf, and Swanstrom 2004; Orfield 1997; Pastor et al. 2000). Are regionalism and asset-based community development compatible? There are several examples of regions adopting the asset-based development approach. In South Central Wisconsin, a newly established regional economic development organization (called Thrive) identified the region's assets and opportunities as part of their strategic planning process (Vandewalle and Associates 2008). On the basis of their analysis, they identified several key assets on which they could build, including the biotechnology and health-care industries, the bio-economy, and others. The advantage in mapping assets on a regional scale is that it recognizes that assets have a broader impact than on a single neighborhood or community, and that they may contribute to economic and social well-being throughout the region. For example, there may be other businesses that are linked to these industries. Similarly, workers for these industries may commute throughout the region.

There may be difficulty in implementing a regionwide-asset approach, however, because some communities may not benefit as much from investments in these assets as others. This is especially the case for economic development. If a business is located in one community, there may be fewer economic benefits for other communities in the region. In other instances, one community may carry the majority of costs for a project (such as an art museum or theater) while residents throughout the region may benefit without paying any costs. These examples demonstrate that the beneficiaries of community assets do not correspond to political boundaries. We need a much better understanding of how regions can manage their assets fairly. What types of institutional changes are needed? Do we need a different set of processes to map assets on a regional basis? What difficulties do we face in mobilizing assets on a regional level?

Conclusions

For much of its history, the field of community development has been shaped by its focus on social problems. Saul Alinsky's work influenced generations of community organizers. Alinsky developed numerous tactics to organize residents around local problems. His assumption was that the lack of power was the primary source of most of the problems faced by communities. The focus, then, is gaining access to external resources or changing power relations between residents and outside organizations and agencies. Organizing residents around problems empowered communities to solve their problems.

The asset-based development model discussed in this book has some important similarities and differences with the Alinksy-style of organizing. Both may emphasize the importance of power and mobilizing residents to improve their quality of life. The well-publicized success of the Dudley Street Neighborhood Initiative (DSNI) in Boston demonstrates how poor neighborhoods can organize around their own assets to build community (Medoff and Sklar 1994). The DSNI diverged from Alinsky's tactics by taking control of key resources—in this case land—to further the goals of the community. This case demonstrates that it is more empowering to mobilizing communities around their resources and assets than it is to focus on the problems in the communities. The case studies reviewed here suggest that although there continue to be challenges to this approach, there are some long-term benefits to organizing residents in this manner.

The distinction that is often drawn between mobilizing local resources versus pressuring powerful systematic forces, however, may be a false one (Kretzmann 2003). Most community development practitioners recognize the value of mixing strategies and modifying processes to meet local needs. Asset-based development may be enhanced by recognizing how structural forces shape opportunities and constraints. Many of the case studies reviewed here focused on internal resources, but recognized the need to address these structural forces in order to be successful.

One of the most important changes in the field of community development over the past fifteen years has been the shift in how external organizations and institutions relate to communities. Not only have communities and practitioners embraced asset-based development principles, but organizations and institutions have modified their practices along these lines as well. Foundations, government agencies, and nonprofit organizations providing technical assistance, training, and funding have a better understanding today of how they can build community capacity without creating dependencies. This does not mean that external agencies and organizations no longer provide technical assistance or offer resources without strings. Instead, many agencies and institutions recognize the importance of communities establishing a strong organizational base, a solid action plan, and a strategy for broad community participation. These basic conditions do not dictate the substantive goals or undermine independence, but enhance the ability of communities to identify, mobilize, and manage their assets more effectively.

By pointing to some of the important successes of asset-based community development over the past two decades, I am not suggesting that most poor communities do not face significant challenges. The working class and the poor have fallen further behind as a result of global economic changes. Residents in poor neighborhoods are still trying to "swim against the tide" against federal and state policies that undermine the capacity of communities (O'Connor 1999). Our only hope is to build stronger and more resilient communities that can challenge these powerful political and economic forces.

References

Dreier, Peter, John Mollenkopf, and Todd Swanstrom. 2004. *Place Matters: Metropolitics for the Twenty-First Century.* Lawrence: University of Kansas Press.

Flora, Jan L., Gary P. Green, Edward A. Gale, Frederick E. Schmidt, and Cornelia Butler Flora. 1992. "Self-development: A viable rural development option?" *Policy Studies Journal* 20:276–288.

Goe, W. Richard, and Gary Paul Green. 2005. "Amenities and change in the well-being of nonmetropolitan localities." Pp. 95–112 in *Amenities and Rural Development: Theory, Methods, and Public Policy,* edited by Gary Paul Green, Steven C. Deller, and David W. Marcouiller. Cheltenham, U.K. and Northhampton, MA: Edward Elgar Publishing.

Green, Gary Paul. 2001. "Amenities and community economic development." *Journal of Regional Analysis and Policy* 31:61–76.

Green, Gary P., Jan L. Flora, Cornelia B. Flora, and Frederick E. Schmidt. 1990. "Local self-development strategies: National survey results." *Journal of the Community Development Society* 21:55–73.

Green, Gary Paul, and Anna Haines. 2007. *Asset Building and Community Development,* 2nd Edition. Thousand Oaks, CA: Sage Publications.

Green, Gary Paul, Anna Haines, and Steve Halebsky. 2000. *Building Our Future: A Guide to Community Visioning.* Madison: University of Wisconsin-Extension.

Kretzmann, John. 2003. "Asset-based community development." Pp. 67–68 in *Encyclopedia of Community,* edited by Karen Christenson and David Levinson. Thousand Oaks, CA: Sage Publications.

Kretzmann, John., and McKnight, John. 1993. *Building Communities from the Inside Out: A Path Toward Finding and Mobilizing a Community's Assets.* Evanston, IL: Center for Urban Affairs and Policy Research, Northwestern University.

Medoff, Peter, and Holly Sklar. 1994. *Streets of Hope.* Boston, MA: South End Press.

O'Connor, Alice. 1999. "Swimming against the tide: A brief history of federal policy in poor communities." Pp. 77–138 in *Urban Problems and Community Development,* edited by Ronald F. Ferguson and William T. Dickens. Washington, DC: Brookings Institution Press.

Orfield, Myron. 1997. *Metropolitics: A Regional Agenda for Community and Stability.* Washington, DC: Brookings Institution Press.

Pastor, Manuel, Peter Dreier, J. Eugene Grigsby III, and Marta Lopez-Garza. 2000. *Regions that Work: How Cities and Suburbs Can Grow Together.* Minneapolis: University of Minnesota Press.

Power, Thomas M. 1996. *Lost Landscapes and Failed Economies: The Search for a Value of Place.* Washington, DC: Island Press.

Vandewalle and Associates. 2008. *Madison Region's Assets and Opportunities Initiative.* Retrieved on February 5, 2009. www.thrivehere.org/asset sandopps.

Warren, Mark R. 2001. *Dry Bones Rattling: Community Building to Revitalize American Democracy.* Princeton, NJ: Princeton University Press.

Contributors

Lionel J. (Bo) Beaulieu is Director of the Southern Rural Development Center at Mississippi State University and a professor in the Department of Agricultural Economics.

Emily Blejwas received her Masters Degree in the Department of Agricultural Economics and Rural Sociology at Auburn University. She now lives in Montgomery, Alabama.

Sarah Dewees is Director of Research for First Nations Development Institute. First Nations Development Institute is a national Native-American-led nonprofit 501(c)(3) development organization that promotes asset-based economic-development strategies for Native American communities. Sarah has managed and evaluated several small-grant programs that support community development financial institutions in Native American communities, and has over fifteen years of experience working in Native and rural communities. Sarah received her Ph.D. in rural sociology from the University of Kentucky in 1998, an M.A. in sociology from Ohio University in 1992, and a B.A. in government from Oberlin College in 1990. She lives with her husband and son in Virginia.

Michael L. Dougherty is a Ph.D. candidate in the Development Studies Program and a research assistant in the Department of Rural Sociology at the University of Wisconsin-Madison. Since 2001 Michael has worked in Guatemala, Nicaragua, and El Salvador as a development practitioner, nonprofit manager, and researcher. His work centers on globalization and development, political economy, and community development in Latin America and the United States. Michael's writing appears in *Journal of the Community Development Society* and *Global Studies Journal*, among others.

Ann Goetting acquired her formal education primarily in Michigan and has been teaching at Western Kentucky University for more than thirty years. She has authored about forty articles in scholarly journals and three books, mostly in the areas of crime, family structure and dynamics, or both. Recently she has served as editor of *Network News* (the newsletter for Sociologists for Women in Society) and *Humanity & Society*. For nearly fifteen years she has concentrated her work in the area of battering and has served as expert witness for approximately twenty battered women charged with some kind of felony behavior (usually murder). Dr. Goetting is an active volunteer for the Bowling Green Warren County Humane society.

Gary Paul Green is a professor in the Department of Community and Environmental Sociology at the University of Wisconsin-Madison and a community development specialist in the Center for Community & Economic Development at the University of Wisconsin-Extension. Green's applied research, teaching, and outreach interests focus on community, economic, and workforce development. His recent books include *Asset Building and Community Development*, 2nd edition (Sage Publications, 2007); *Workforce Development Networks in Rural Areas* (Edward Elgar Publishing, 2007); and *Amenities and Rural Development* (Edward Elgar Publishing, 2005).

Mark H. Harvey is an assistant professor in the Department of Sociology at Florida Atlantic University. Mark received his Ph.D. at the University of Wisconsin-Madison. He recently published *Welfare Reform in Persistent Rural Poverty: Dreams, Disenchantments, and Diversity* (Penn State Press, 2006).

John (Jody) P. Kretzmann is Codirector of the Asset-Based Community Development (ABCD) Institute, a research project of the Institute for Policy Research at Northwestern University. He was a founding faculty member of the Associated Colleges of the Midwest (ACM) Urban Studies Program in 1969, and served as director of that institution for six years. He has been a community organizer in Chicago's west side, and served as a consultant to a wide range of neighborhood organizing and development groups. In addition to the ACM program, he has taught at Northwestern University, Valparaiso University, and the Lutheran School of Theology in Chicago.

Rocío Peralta is an architect and environmental scientist. She has advanced degrees from the Universidad del Valle, Guatemala, and the Universidad de San Pablo CEU in Seville, Spain. Rocío works as an environmental consultant in Guatemala. She specializes in protected-area management, environmental impact studies, disaster management, and gender issues.

Rhonda Phillips, AICP, CEcD, is a professor of community development with Arizona State University's School of Community Resources & Development. Her work in cultural-based development includes Artful Business, a forum on arts-based development strategies for community revitalization, and she is the author of *Concept Marketing for Communities* (Praeger, 2002), which chronicles arts-based economic-development strategies.

Deborah Puntenney is Associate Director of the Asset-Based Community Development Institute and a member of the research faculty at Northwestern University, and a member of the adjunct faculty at the University of Chicago. She also consults with nonprofit organizations in the areas of community research and evaluation as well as social justice.

Stewart Sarkozy-Banoczy is Vice President and Chief Operating Officer for the Oweesta Corporation (www.oweesta.org), which is the only certified national Native community development financial institution (CDFI) intermediary in the United States. Before joining Oweesta, Stewart was the organizer and founding Executive Director of Four Bands Community Fund, Inc. (www.fourbands.org), a Native CDFI on the Cheyenne River Lakota Reservation in South Dakota. Stewart worked as an administrator and entrepreneurship instructor at Si Tanka, the tribal college on the Cheyenne River Reservation. He has also worked on business-development projects in Russia, Germany, England, and Mexico. In June of 2004 Stewart was awarded the Appel Prize for Entrepreneurial Vitality from the Price-Babson College Fellows Program as part of the Symposium for Entrepreneurship Educators. Stewart has an M.B.A in International Management from the Thunderbird School of Global Management. He lives with his wife, Jody, and their two children in the Black Hills of South Dakota.

Gordon Shockley is an assistant professor of Social Entrepreneurship and a faculty associate of the Lodestar Center for Philanthropy and Nonprofit Innovation at Arizona State University. His research interests span nonmarket entrepreneurship, public policy analysis, and the politics, economics, and sociology of the arts and humanities. He earned a Ph.D. in public policy from George Mason University; an M.M. from the J.L. Kellogg Graduate School of Management, Northwestern University; and a B.A. in Ancient Greek and English Languages and Literature from the University of California, Los Angeles. He also has several years of public service at all levels of the U.S. government.

 Index